W9-CBA-448

This book is an invitation—an invitation to join me in proclaiming and living out the gospel in a way that brings good news to the poor and liberty to the oppressed. It is an invitation to white and black, Jew and Gentile, to every racial and ethnic group in our nation to be reconciled to one another, to work together to make our land all God wants it to be. And it is a blueprint—a practical strategy by which American evangelicals can do the work of biblical justice in our own land.

Just as Nehemiah challenged his countrymen to join him in rebuilding the wall of Jerusalem, I extend my challenge to you—my fellow country-men, my fellow Christians: Come, let us rebuild the wall of America!

John M. Perkins

WITH JUSTICE FOR ALL

JOHN PERKINS
Foreword by Chuck Colson

Regal Books
A Division of GL Publications
Ventura, CA U.S.A.

The foreign language publishing of all Regal books is under the direction of Gospel Literature International (GLINT). GLINT provides financial and technical help for the adaptation, translation and publishing of books for millions of people worldwide. For information regarding translation, contact: GLINT, P.O. Box 6688, Ventura, California 93006.

Published by Regal Books
A Division of GL Publications
Ventura, California 93006

Printed in U.S.A.

Library of Congress Cataloging in Publication Data
Perkins, John, 1930-
    With justice for all.
      1. Christianity and justice—United States.
2. Church and social problems—United States.   3. United States—Moral conditions.   4. Perkins, John, 1930-
I. Title.
BR115.J8P47   261.8   80-50262
ISBN 0-8307-0754-9   AACR2

To
Derek Perkins, my third son,
and Don Strohnbehn,
and
the four young men at Harambee House:
Philip "Pogo" Brown
Willie Cavett
Perry Davis
and Billy Ray Stokes
who to me represent
the future leaders
of the Jackson community

CONTENTS

Foreword

John Perkins is a prophet. He is also a loving brother and friend. As a matter of fact, in my very first encounter with him, he taught me one of the most important lessons of my Christian life.

I had come to Jackson, Mississippi to speak at a rally sponsored by John's ministry. It was the first time that Voice of Calvary, primarily a black ministry, had staged a public event seeking to involve the largely white population of Jackson. John hoped that my speaking would break down century-old barriers.

I had been in Jackson a year earlier for the Governor's Prayer Breakfast. There was an overflow crowd of over 2,000. Hundreds had wanted tickets but could not get in.

But in sharp contrast, when I arrived in the auditorium for the Voice of Calvary rally there were more empty chairs than I had ever seen in my life. Four or five hundred of John's supporters were sitting in the front, and throughout the rest of the cavernous auditorium I could see only little islands of people—maybe 100 at the most—from the local white community.

As a white man I was embarrassed and hurt for my new friend, John. He could tell that I was angry; he leaned over to me and said, "Don't worry about it, brother; it will all be all right in God's timing." Here was a man who had been beaten and tortured during the civil rights movement in the sixties. Though he might have been bitter again this night, he instead radiated God's love.

That is the kind of man John Perkins is, and *With Justice for All* communicates that same spirit of love and commitment to Christ. This book is not just another theoretical treatise or cold-blooded analysis of the fabric of American culture. Woven throughout it are examples of God's working in John's life and ministry over the last 20 years, with practical principles drawn from Scripture. When John describes his work as a blueprint, it is a plan I trust because of his dependence on Scripture and his practical experience. As the "Ten Years Later" chapter makes clear, John's work is not an untried philosophical supposition, nor has it been a series of easy victories. His principles of relocation, reconciliation and redistribution have been tried by fire. Suffering has been an intrinsic part of his personal experience; his resulting wisdom is hard won. As he likens the leaders American Christians so desperately need to Nehemiah, he is serving as an example. John Perkins is a voice shouting out in the wilderness of contemporary modern culture; now, more than ever before, we need to heed that call.

If effective, deep-seated change is to come to our nation today, it will come only through the leadership of Christians—not as a political force, but as a network of believers sharing the reconciling love of Jesus Christ and the power of His gospel to meet the gamut of men and women's moral, physical, spiritual and emotional needs.

As we see the power of that gospel communicated through the believing hearts and practical actions of Christians ministering in the weak places of our society, we will see committed Christian fellowships growing among the poor and oppressed in our ghettos, reconciliation between black and white in our cities, healing of the broken within our prisons. Though it may seem to be foolishness to the world, it will be from the ranks of the powerless that the powerful see the work of Christ.

As John Perkins makes clear, this work begins with you and me. As we ourselves have feasted on the good news, we must in turn proclaim liberty to the captives and justice to the oppressed. As Christ ministers through us, then we will begin to see healing in our land—not through government programs or distant relief funds, but by rolling up our shirt sleeves, taking on the concerns of the needy and sharing in their sufferings. This is the model Christ gives us—and it is leaders like John Perkins who show the excellence of their leadership by focusing our eyes on Christ.

Charles W. Colson

ACKNOWLEDGEMENTS

I would like to express special thanks to Eddy Hall for his good editorial work, and to my wife, Vera Mae, who worked with me on this book. Thanks also go to Sue Nelson who spent hour after hour retyping this book with some assistance from Melody Hall. The research of Tom Adams, Eva Meiers, and Joannie Perkins was much appreciated. I am grateful to Tim Robertson for letting me borrow heavily from a sermon he delivered to Voice of Calvary Fellowship in December of 1980 for most of the material included in chapter 19. Thank you to Steven Crane, Margaret Love Denman, Tim Robertson, H. Spees, Lem Tucker, and Sue Nelson for reading the manuscript and offering helpful suggestions. A special thanks to Donna Wheeler, my secretary, without whose help I would never have had the time to write this book. I want to thank Bill Greig, Jr., president of GL Publications, who encouraged me to write this book.

I am also grateful to the entire Denman family: to Rusty and Margaret Love for giving us free access to their home, to their meat locker, to the fruit trees around their farm, and to their lives during the weeks we spent drafting the manuscript; to all of the wonderful Denman kids—Pepper, Laura, John, Stanton, and Hunter—for helping to make us welcome during our stay; and especially to Pepper, Laura, and John, who moved out of their beautiful three-bedroom home to make room for us.

Thanks to Jim and Shirley Posey for opening their home to Vera Mae and me during the final editing of the manuscript.

Finally, I want to thank the many friends who encouraged us and helped us in many other ways while working on this project.

Introduction

"We hold these truths to be self-evident, that all men are created equal . . ." With these words the Declaration of Independence of the United States of America holds out the noble promise of justice for all. Yet the very signing of this landmark of human freedom betrayed its own promise. For among its signers stood men who at that very moment owned other men. Justice for all didn't really mean justice for *all;* it meant justice for some. The "inalienable" right of liberty belonged only to the privileged.

To this day our nation has not lived up to its goal of justice for all. Would anyone claim that a child trapped in the ghetto has equal access to quality education as his suburban counterpart? Would anyone claim that the teenage girl in the ghetto has the same chance of getting a summer job as the girl from an affluent family? Or that the ethnic young adult, deprived of good education and job experience, has an equal chance of making it in the American job market?

Poverty, you see, is much more than lack of money; *poverty is the lack of options.* For millions in our land there is not justice. For them, "equal opportunity" is at best an elusive dream; at worst a cruel taunt.

But this is not a book of despair; it is a book of hope. Though our nation has failed to live up to its own ideal of justice, I believe it can. I believe that justice for all can become a reality in America. Government alone though, however good, can never bring justice. I am convinced that the promise which our nation's laws alone have been powerless to fulfill can only be fulfilled in one way—through the power of the gospel of Jesus Christ.

Yes, the gospel has this power. I know, for I have seen it bring hope to the hopeless; I have seen it empower the powerless to break the chains of oppression.

I am persuaded that the church, as the steward of this gospel, holds the key to justice in our society. Either justice will come through us or it will not come at all.

About three years ago I tried to challenge the Gospel Light staff with the urgency of this mission. After I spoke, Bill Greig, the president, came up to me. "John," he suggested, "why don't you follow up *Let Justice Roll Down* with a book that explains how we Christians in America can work for biblical justice? We'll call it *With Justice for All.*

As the months passed, I became more and more convinced that the book was needed. I watched the American evangelical church mushroom in numbers while losing the battle against crime and immorality. The church was not transforming our society. The Moral Majority emerged and made a political statement—maybe a needed statement—yet one that ignored the plight of the disenfranchised. I began to wonder if conservative evangelicals were making the same grave error the liberals had made—seeking political solutions to moral problems.

Watergate. Koreagate. Abscam. Skyrocketing crime rates. They all added to my sense of urgency. Christians need to act—now! And so, this book. This book is an invitation—an invitation to join me in proclaiming and living out the gospel in a way that brings good news to the poor and liberty to the oppressed (see Luke 4:18). It is an invitation to white and black, Jew and Gentile, to every racial and ethnic group in our nation to be reconciled to one another, to work together to make our land all God wants it to be. And it is a blueprint—a practical strategy by which American evangelicals can do the work of biblical justice in our own land.

When I attend the World Vision board meetings I am bombarded by the cries and suffering of the people of the world. In the face of such overwhelming need I feel utterly helpless.

Yet I know where we have to start. To correct economic injustice, we must pursue a strategy of development— empowering people to become self-sufficient through the power of the gospel. Yes, the very lives of the victims of famine and war depend on our relief efforts. We dare not neglect those needs. But the greater need is for development—to break the cycle of poverty, so that today's receivers become tomorrow's givers.

The growing social awareness in American evangelical churches encourages me. Some of our largest congregations are raising big offerings for overseas hospitals or giving other compassionate responses to the needy. That is good. But it is not enough. Far more than they need our money, the poor need us—people. People with skills who will work with them and teach them how to become self-sufficient.

This book maps a strategy for just that kind of development. It is my attempt to share what God has taught me about ministry. Because God usually teaches me through real life experiences, this book is full of stories from my life. Naturally, many of the stories in this book have been told before in *Let Justice Roll Down* and *A Quiet Revolution*. Unlike *Let Justice Roll Down*, however, which tells my life story, these events are not all in chronological order. I tell each story to share with you how God first taught me some ministry principle, or to illustrate that principle.

To help you to personalize the ministry principles, "Reflection" questions for personal or group study follow each chapter. For groups ready to move beyond talking about justice to doing justice, instructions for six "Interaction" sessions are included, at the end of the book. These are so designed that visitors to the group who have not read the book can participate in all the activities, making these activities suitable for such groups as a Sunday School class or an open small group.

The first three chapters lay out the need for such a strategy—why evangelism is not enough, and how both white evangelicals and the black church have failed to rise to the challenge of biblical justice in America.

Chapters 4 and 5 describe how God nurtured within me the dream for Voice of Calvary, then gave me a strategy to do what He had called me to do. I call this strategy the "Three *Rs* of Christian community development"—relocation, reconciliation, and redistribution.

The first *R* is *relocation*.

To be an effective community developer I must relocate into the community of need. I must live among those I am serving. I must become one of them. Their needs must become my needs. Chapter 6 illustrates this principle.

Chapter 7 reports how over our 20-year ministry we have raised up indigenous leaders from the community who can take over the work of Christian community development. Chapter 8 explores the role of volunteers at Voice of Calvary and the value of the volunteering experience. Chapter 9 suggests specific practical steps for applying the principle of relocation.

The second *R* is *reconciliation*.

In an incredible night of horrors I was beaten to within an inch of my life by policemen in Brandon, Mississippi. It was as I was being beaten that I heard and accepted God's call to a ministry of reconciliation between blacks and whites. Chapter 10 tells that story. Chapters 11 and 12 report our efforts to do the work of reconciliation through a new ministry in Jackson, Mississippi's capital. Chapter 13 reviews the fruits of VOC's 20 years of ministry in the heart of racially torn Mississippi. The final chapter of this section offers practical suggestions for implementing this principle.

The third *R* is *redistribution*.

The earth does not belong to you and me, but to God. We are only its stewards. God provided the earth for all mankind. Economic injustice, then, is simply depriving people of free access to God's creation. Justice is achieved by working with God to share His resources with the disenfranchised of the earth. Chapter 15 examines the demand of justice to redistribute the resources of our nation.

Chapter 16, "The Not-So-Great Society," notes the failure of government social welfare programs to achieve redistribution. Today it is popular to oppose government welfare programs because they are too expensive. That is not why I oppose them. My objection is that these programs victimize the very people they are designed to help. Though conceived in compassion, most of the poverty programs do not develop people, but cripple them. In this chapter I propose a fundamental change in government's role in helping the poor.

Chapter 17 shows how we can make our free enterprise system work for us through cooperative economic development in poor communities. Chapter 18 offers additional practical guidelines for achieving redistribution.

Finally, this strategy of Christian community development calls for effective leaders. What kind of leader can be effective in this task? Nehemiah, by his example, paints a powerful picture of just such a leader.

Just as Nehemiah challenged his countrymen to join him in rebuilding the wall of Jerusalem, I extend my challenge to you—my fellow countrymen, my fellow Christians: Come, let us rebuild the wall of America!

THE NEED

1. Evangelism Is Not Enough
2. A Powerless Gospel
3. Sheep Without a Shepherd

1

EVANGELISM IS
NOT ENOUGH

It was one of the best things that ever happened to me. It seemed to come out of the blue. I had no inkling that it was coming before that Sunday afternoon in the fall of 1961. That was the day I got kicked out of the church.

Just my being in that little church in Mendenhall, Mississippi wasn't exactly my idea. I had left the state at age 17—for good. Or so I thought. Coming back was the last thing I wanted to do.

You see, back then blacks in rural Mississippi had three choices: we could stay, accept the system and become dehumanized niggers; we could go to jail or get killed; or we could leave for the big city. For my family it didn't seem safe to stay, so most of us made off for California.

Growing up for me wasn't filled with the kind of fond memories that might make me want to go back home. Momma died a slow, painful death of pellagra when I was seven months old, from lack of milk and medical care. About the time Momma died my father left home and gave all of us kids—Clyde, Mary, Clifton, Emma Jean and me—to his mother. Grandma Perkins—Aunt Babe, people called her—had already raised 19 kids of her own. In time she had to give three of us kids away. She kept me because I was little and sickly. She kept Clyde too, because he was big enough to plow.

We were sharecroppers. Sharecroppers and bootleggers. We lived on Mr. Bush's plantation in a three-room shack with our aunts and uncles and cousins. There were always at least 12 of us, sometimes as many as 15 living there.

During my teens, tragedy struck my family repeatedly. Mary's boyfriend killed her in Louisiana. I never knew the details. Then Clyde got shot by a deputy marshall. He rode in my arms to the hospital in Jackson, 50 miles away. A few hours later he died. Other members of my family were killed too, all within just a few years. Bitterness and hatred ate at me. That's when I left Mississippi. I was going to put all that behind me once and for all.

In California I found all kinds of new opportunities. I got a good job at Union Pacific Foundry in South Gate and soon was organizing the work of the men on the production line. When we joined the United Steel Workers Union, although I was still a teen, I was chosen our department's union steward. Before long I was in the thick of organizing a strike which won us several benefits, including a piecework provision that sometimes brought me as much as $100 a week—not bad money for back then. I've never forgotten the power of united action.

In the spring of 1957 the gospel of Jesus Christ confronted me. By then I had been through the Korean War, gotten married to Vera Mae, and started a family. My oldest son Spencer was going to the weekly Good News Clubs at a little church just down the street from our house. Spencer started coming home and saying verses before we began to eat—something we had never done before. I watched Spencer. I saw something beautiful developing in him, something I knew nothing about. Never before had I seen Christianity really work in anyone's life.

Before long I joined my wife and children in attending a little church in Pasadena which plainly taught the Word of God. Here I joined a class that was studying the life of Paul. I had never taken the Bible seriously before. I had always thought of it as a bunch of old wives' tales and superstitions. But now I was eager to learn. This Paul really intrigued me. What made him tick? What motivated this man to suffer so much for a religion? If he had been going after money I could have understood him. But religion! How could religion mean so much to anybody, even Paul? The question hounded me all summer.

The answer came as I grappled with Paul's message of law and grace. In Galatians 2:20, Paul wrote, "I am crucified with Christ: nevertheless I live; yet not I, but Christ liveth in me; and the life which I now live in the flesh I live by the faith of the Son of God, who loved me, and gave himself for me" *(KJV)*. At age 27, for the first time in my life, I came to see that the Christian life was more than what I was seeing in the churches. It was the outliving of the in-living Christ! I knew Christ wasn't living inside me. I felt a deep inner hunger to know Him in this personal way.

One Sunday morning the minister spoke from Romans 6:23: "The wages of sin is death; but the gift of God is eternal life through Jesus Christ our Lord" *(KJV)*. For the first time I saw that I was a sinner. I saw that I was committing my every act of sin against a holy God who loved me and had sent His Son to die for me. That morning I accepted the gift of eternal life. A joy filled my life. I felt just as though that was the day for which I had been born.

I started growing in my new life. I studied this mystery of God's great love for me and His forgiveness for my sins. My church family nourished me in the Word. The director of Child Evangelism Fellowship for the San Gabriel Valley, Mr. Wayne Leitch, began to teach me. Hour after hour, day after day, he faithfully ministered the Word to me. Two days a week, an hour and a half each day, he taught me, for two years until he had led me from Genesis through Revelation.

I began to share this newfound joy with others. I rounded up children and brought them into my home to tell them about Jesus. There were about 28 of them, many of them young boys—boys who didn't go to Sunday School, boys much like I had been.

I began going with some Christian businessmen to share my testimony with the young prisoners in the prison camps along the San Dimas Mountains. One morning as I told how I had dropped out of school between the third and fifth grades, and how God had come into my life and transformed it, two young men broke down and cried. After the session, I talked with them. They told me that their lives were much like mine and that they too wanted to know Christ.

As those boys shared their life stories with me it started me thinking about my own values and goals. Many of them had backgrounds just like mine. Some came from the deep South or were the children of families who came from there. They came to California just as I did, but for some reason they hadn't "made it."

Many of the problems in the ghetto, I was seeing, were really the unsolved problems of the South. This incident triggered a growing conviction that God wanted me to go back to Mississippi to identify with my people there, to help them break out of the cycle of despair—not by encouraging them to leave but by showing them new life right where they were.

An inner battle raged for the next two years. On the one hand I had a growing hunger to go back to Mississippi and share this newfound love of God with my people. On the other hand I was afraid. We were just beginning to make it. After the Korean War I started with another company as janitor and worked up into a leadership position. I was motivated. I loved my job. What I really loved, I think, was the result of working—the money. I saved money and bought stock in the company. My stock divided twice while I worked there. I bought a big 12-room house to raise my growing family. I was all set.

The lines of battle were drawn. Which would it be—the values of the world or sharing God's Word in Mississippi?

I already had definite goals and was working hard to reach them. I didn't want to give those up. So I worked all the harder on my job, trying to drown out this call. But it wouldn't go away.

Another reason I didn't want to go was that I realized I was inadequate. One night I had this incredible dream. I dreamed that I was preaching to a whole crowd of people in front of my house. That was really something—me preaching to all those people! Here I was a third grade dropout. *No way* would I ever be preaching to all those people! And so I kept rejecting the call.

I remember when my growing conviction became a command. I was giving my testimony to a church in Arcadia, California. My text came from Romans 10:1,2: "Brethren, my heart's desire and prayer to God for Israel is, that they might be saved. For I bear them record that they have a zeal of God, but not according to knowledge" *(KJV)*.

God took the power of Paul's love for His people and shot it through me saying, "John, my desire for you is that you go back to Mississippi, because I bear your people witness that they have a zeal for God, but it is not enlightened."

I was reminded of the emotionalism of many of the congregations I had seen and heard. I thought of how little my people really knew about the Bible. It was true. My people had a zeal for God but not according to knowledge.

God was calling me. I could never be at home in California after that.

June 9, 1960, saw us arrive back in Mississippi—the same Mississippi I had once left "for good." Vera Mae and I and our five children went to live with her grandmother down near New Hebron. During that summer we organized some vacation Bible schools. In the fall I started holding chapels in the public schools. Before long I was reaching about 15 thousand kids a month over a five-county area. I also became the regular chaplain at Prentiss Institute, a black junior college. God was opening doors.

In February of 1961 we found a house in Mendenhall, 17 miles away. I liked the location because Mendenhall was near the center of my area of ministry. Although our new house was right across the street from the Nazareth Baptist Church, every Sunday Vera Mae and I still drove back down to the Oak Ridge Church in New Hebron. Pretty soon, though, we saw that it made more sense to worship in Mendenhall and we made the change.

The people at the Mendenhall church had heard about me so they asked me to be a guest teacher in the Sunday School class. They really enjoyed my teaching. This new open door really excited me because I saw it as an opportunity for evangelism. Evangelism was my one burning concern. I wanted to win people to Jesus Christ! I believed that if people would come to know Christ their lives would be changed and everything would be okay. That belief, though, was about to be challenged.

The blacks in Mendenhall all lived across the tracks in "the quarters," the section of town that had years before been set aside for slaves. As I walked the dirt streets in the quarters (only the "uptown" streets were paved), I passed shack after shack. The paint had long since peeled off most of the houses. Porches dropped. One makeshift room after another clung to the houses where they had been added to make room for growing families. The plumbing consisted of a lone water faucet beside each shack. A honky-tonk, a room attached to the side of a house and boasting a Coca-Cola sign above the door, graced each end of the street.

Poverty's smells hung in the air. A strong blend of backyard pigpens, outhouses, and cow manure being burned as mosquito bombs on front porches was joined at supper time with the aroma of good Southern cooking.

People sat listlessly on their porches, their hopeless faces haunting me. At every house, it seemed, someone was sick. Children dogged my steps, begging for pennies. I didn't yet realize that practically all of them had been born out of wedlock, then left behind with aunts or grandmothers by mothers moving on to the big city.

But of everything I saw, the one thing that most burdened me was the pregnant teenage girls. That year at Harper High alone 17 got pregnant and dropped out of school with little or no prospect of ever going back to finish. In every single school where I worked the story was repeated. With their education cut short, these girls' best chance for rising above their poverty was gone. And the thing that amazed me was which girls were getting pregnant. They weren't the "losers," the unmotivated girls who had already dropped out of school, but the smartest, the most popular, the most promising girls in the schools.

I couldn't understand this until I found out what went on at the five little honky-tonks—quite a few for a town that size. Here kids came to play pinball, listen to records, dance, and drink bootleg whiskey. Since this was the extent of the entertainment in the black community, it was only natural that the most popular girls would go there. An evening of partying would often lead to sexual intercourse and pregnancies.

God was beginning to show me that the gospel had to be

more than just "evangelism." The gospel, rightly understood, is holistic—it responds to man as a whole person; it doesn't single out just spiritual or just physical needs and speak only to those. As Chuck Colson shares:

> A faith . . . which stops with the belief that being "saved" is the whole Christian experience, is dead and denies Christ's concern for all mankind. It is like a baby dying in infancy; the child may be born healthy, but his life will have little or no impact on others.
>
> Grasping this concept was a turning point for me, as it is, I suspect, for many Christians. God, I now understood, was working a powerful transformation in my thought habits and forcing me to *think* about what it really means to live as a disciple of Christ.[1]

Those teenage pregnancies so troubled me that I began to urge my Sunday School class, "Why don't we do something about this? Why don't we try to create a playground? Why don't we get organized, get rid of these honky-tonks, and make life better for our kids?"

I was sure they would see how these juke joints were hurting their kids and want to get rid of them. After all, the number one goal for most families was to get their kids to finish school. Every home proudly displayed on its mantel a picture of the kids that had made it through high school. But for some reason, the people in my class didn't see how this was affecting them. They agreed that there was sin out there, but they didn't see how the church had any responsibility to solve the problem or to create a better environment for their kids.

When I tackled the honky-tonk issue I was in the dark about one critical fact—most of these honky-tonks were owned by members of the church. So here I was, a newcomer in the church, criticizing people who happened to be some of the church's leading givers. To some in my class it came across as slander. So they complained to the pastor.

Now you have to understand that Reverend Morris didn't live in Mendenhall. And because he was pastoring five churches at once he only preached in our church two Sunday evenings a month. When he heard that there was a new man in the community—a preacher, no less—who was talking against some of his members, some of his best members as far as he was concerned, well, he wanted to talk to me.

That Sunday afternoon I came to church early to talk with him. He invited me into his study. We sat down and he looked me in the eye. "Reverend Perkins, some of the church people have come to me. They're upset about your teaching. I wish you wouldn't teach in my church any more."

I was floored. And hurt. I had been so excited about this chance to teach the Word, and now here I was being kicked out of the church!

But like I said, that turned out to be one of the best things that ever happened to me, for out of that closed door Voice of Calvary Ministries was born.

Since I couldn't teach at Nazareth Baptist Church, Vera Mae and I organized a new Sunday School with 17 people. Mrs. Effie Mae Tyler of D'Lo opened her home for Bible classes our first year in Mendenhall. To this day whenever I see her she reminds me that Voice of Calvary Ministries started in her living room.

Within the next two years we built a Jim Walter shell home, one of those where you finish the interior yourself. We lived upstairs and turned the downstairs into a meeting place for Sunday School, Bible classes, and Youth for Christ meetings.

Our third year there we bought six lots and a big tent and held revival meetings. Under that big tent a young man named Dolphus Weary was saved.

Evangelism was happening! But the realities of daily life in rural Mississippi reminded us constantly of what God had taught us during that first crucial year: evangelism is not enough.

REFLECTION

1. What do you think the author means by the statement, "Evangelism is not enough?"
2. What does the author mean by holistic ministry? To what other possible approach or approaches is he contrasting holistic ministry?
3. Was Jesus' ministry holistic? Explain your answer.
4. What implications does the concept of holistic ministry have for your church's approach to ministry? For your own personal ministry?

2

A POWERLESS GOSPEL

I stared ahead into the semicircle of light created by my headlights. The next hill rose to meet me. And then I was easing down into the next hollow. The countryside was sleeping already. Still quietness surrounded me. But inside, turmoil.

I had spent the evening at the Prentiss Extension of the Mississippi Baptist Seminary. The extension was the white seminary's attempt to provide good Bible training to black preachers. At the invitation of the dean, Mr. S. L. Richmond, I had spoken that night in chapel to an audience of black students sprinkled with the handful of white pastors and professors who taught there.

The chorus of "Amens" and "Hallelujahs" that usually greet a black sermon was absent that night. As I spread before them a story of God's mighty acts from the Word, an eager, intense, amazed attentiveness filled the room. Most had never before seen the Bible come alive through flannelgraph. The power of the story gripped them afresh during those moments.

He came up to me immediately after the presentation. "That was great, John, just great!"

"Thank you, Reverend." This white pastor's enthusiasm

warmed and encouraged me. He led a large, growing congregation—with a beautiful big brick building—just outside of Columbia.

"Yes, John, I really enjoyed that. I wish my people could see that. They would just love it. Could you . . ."

In midair, his sentence hung. His eyes fell. His head dropped. For in his enthusiasm for just an instant he almost forgot that I was black and his church was white. He almost forgot that I could not even attend his church, much less speak there. He almost forgot.

That was the scene that tormented me as I drove the 27 miles back to Mendenhall. I hadn't really expected him to invite me to speak in his church; I knew he couldn't. But in California I had spoken in white churches time and again. I knew it didn't have to be this way.

I thought of the Southern white radio preachers I listened to as I drove this very stretch of road every week going to and from my Prentiss Institute Bible class. They preached exactly what I preached: justification by faith; the blood of Jesus; being born again—all these things. But what difference did it make in their lives? The gospel wasn't changing the way they related to society. For that matter, it wasn't much changing how I related to society either.

I pictured the frequent store window posters: "REVIVAL TONIGHT—EVERYONE WELCOME," with their un-missable, invisible postscript—"EXCEPT BLACKS."

Was the gospel really so irrelevant that it could not challenge hatred and oppression? Was it powerless to bring together even black and white Christians—brothers and sisters in the Lord?

In the days that followed, the streets of Mendenhall constantly confronted me with hunger and poverty, reminders that justice was a stranger there. I recalled the stories of my mother's suffering as she died without milk and medical care. I remembered my brother being shot to death by a deputy marshall in New Hebron. I thought of how my cousin Joe was shot in cold blood, how other blacks were being murdered and nobody was doing anything about it. Where was liberty and justice for all? I could hardly say the pledge of allegiance without the words sticking in my throat.

I couldn't escape this haunting question: Where was the power of the gospel?

I believed in Jesus so much because He had saved me and so transformed my life and given me such a great desire to help others. And I believed the Bible because I had been converted through studying the Bible. I was persuaded that the Bible had something to say about the plight of my people. There just had to be a way for the gospel to become relevant, to burn through these barriers. Somehow the preaching of the gospel had to be able to do that. But it wasn't doing it.

I didn't have a strategy; I only saw the need. The most obvious part of the problem was that whites wanted blacks to be second-class citizens. Black theologian James H. Cone describes this from his own experience of growing up in Bearden, Arkansas:

> White people did everything within their power to define black reality, to tell us who we were—and their definition, of course, extended no further than their social, political, and economic interests. They tried to make us believe that God created black people to be white people's servants. We blacks, therefore, were *expected* to enjoy plowing their fields, cleaning their houses, mowing their lawns, and working in their sawmills. And when we showed signs of displeasure with our so-called elected and inferior status, they called us "uppity niggers" and quickly attempted to put us in our "place."[2]

But that was only half the problem. The other half was that blacks had accepted being second-class citizens. Whenever I would talk to black folks about improving our situation, they would ask, "What would the people uptown think?" The people in Mendenhall had accepted their plight. They were convinced that they could do nothing about it.

When I saw the two-fold nature of the problem, I realized that the solution—whatever it was—had to deal with both whites and blacks. Somehow whites and blacks would have to work together to lick this thing. And that was when I decided to try to get to know Reverend Robert Odenwald, the pastor of the First Baptist Church in Mendenhall.

Seldom before or since have I had to work up so much

courage to do anything. I was tense, but bent on doing it. I went to the church uptown, opened the door, and walked into the church hall. I ran into the black janitor, Willie McGee, and asked him where I could find Reverend Odenwald. Mild horror crossed his face. Probably no black had ever before come there looking for anyone but him.

I walked into the outer office and asked the secretary if the pastor was in. She too looked surprised and bewildered. I waited, my heart in my throat, while she inquired with Reverend Odenwald.

From his study came the words, "Yes, send him in." What relief! What a sense of affirmation, warmth, joy!

In his office, then, I unloaded my heart about the plight of Mendenhall's blacks. We talked quite a while. Then I asked him, "Reverend Odenwald, how do you feel when you go down into the quarters and pick up your maid? When you see black kids on the street, barefooted, when they ought to be in school? How do you feel when you hear about the crime, the school dropouts, the theft? And when you realize that these little kids are the ones who in a few years will be doing that?"

He leaned over in his seat, listening more intently.

"How do you feel," I went on, "when you think about your elaborate church building with its beautiful chandeliers, when you realize that your denomination is supporting missionaries in Africa and all the time right here in Mendenhall are people who have never really heard the gospel of Jesus Christ?"

I could tell he was moved. He really wanted to help us.

He began to ask me theological questions. I realized he wanted to see if I was a real Bible-believing preacher. He wanted to see if I might really have a solution or if I only knew the problem. He asked me about justification by faith, and I quoted verses like Ephesians 2:8 and 9, "For by grace are ye saved through faith . . ." *(KJV).* We talked about dispensationalism, amillennialism, premillennialism, and more. He was astonished that a black knew that much about the Bible.

He then told me that he had grown up on a plantation. My telling him about the needs of the black people reminded him of the people he had known as he was growing up in the Delta. He identified with my work and felt a heavy burden for it.

He gave me a book he had read about a black minister named John Jasper. Jasper was a well-known preacher around the time of the Emancipation. He was working in a tobacco factory when he got converted. He began to preach in that tobacco factory and in the slave quarters on Sunday. His master eventually sent him off with the words, "Preach the Word, John, preach the Word."

Reverend Odenwald turned to me there in his study and seemed to reenact that historical event. "Preach the Word, John," he said. "Preach the Word."

I felt that he was saying something profound. He was saying, "I can't free them but you can." I had gone there to get some kind of charity. When I left, I think he felt he hadn't helped me much, and I hadn't gotten the kind of help I needed. But he had given me something far more valuable than charity—he had helped me accept the responsibility to free my people.

For the next two Sundays Reverend Odenwald presented the plight of the black community to his congregation. He voiced the contradiction he had seen between biblical truth and the social attitudes he and his congregation accepted unthinkingly from the surrounding white society. But his people turned their backs on him.

I could tell this man was under tremendous stress, but I never understood at the time all he was going through. One night as I was driving along that same stretch of road from Prentiss to Mendenhall, the news came over the radio— Reverend Odenwald had committed suicide. And there was more to come.

I remember one day when Vera Mae and I went up to visit another white pastor, a good friend who had built a large Presbyterian church in another city. While attending Dallas Theological Seminary he had taught classes at Dallas Bible Training School where black preachers were trained. There he had developed a deep love and concern for blacks. When he came to the Mississippi Delta he found that neither his church nor the black church was doing anything about the poverty in the area. So he persuaded his church to set aside $3,000 a year toward starting a black ministry there. We had been helping him to lay the groundwork for this new ministry.

Well, on this day we visited and talked about the ministry until noon rolled around. Since we were his guests it was only natural that we would go to lunch together. Except we couldn't. The civil rights movement was in full swing. In fact, in that very town a boycott was being held because blacks were trying to integrate some of the cafes. He couldn't invite us home with him either, because both his wife and the people in the community would object. So he gave us five dollars to eat lunch on our own while he went home to eat.

At one o'clock we came back and continued our conversation. My friend was in turmoil. When we left that day, he was in tears.

Some time later we got the news. He too had committed suicide.

Now that made me take a good hard look at what was happening to the church in Mississippi. Here were two compassionate pastors, rays of hope in a sea of darkness who had wanted to reach out to others. But they had suffered such rejection from their own people that they took their own lives.

I was sharing with other black pastors my concern that we weren't making any difference in the condition of those we pastored. As they began to catch a vision for the church's responsibility, I noticed that they too began to have emotional problems.

I began to see that white and black churches alike had so molded their message to fit within cultural, racial and religious traditions that they had robbed the gospel of its power. It was powerless to reach across racial, cultural, economic and social barriers. It could not make a real difference in the community.

I, like my fellow pastors, felt torn between my commitment to justice and my commitment to the church. On the one hand was the civil rights movement, now in full swing. It was attracting the loyalty of thousands of young people who loved the idea of freedom, but most of whom had at best only a shallow faith in Jesus Christ. They were more concerned about the movement than the things of the Lord.

On the other side was the evangelical church. Almost all the evangelicals I knew opposed the movement. The evangelical church seemed to have no room for social justice.

My heart was torn between my evangelical friends and my commitment to the suffering and agony of my people. It seemed that I could not have both.

Here was a movement for social justice which held the potential to bring us all together, to live out the gospel in a way that would finally make a difference. To do that the movement needed evangelical leadership. I wanted to be part of that leadership. But I was trapped by a "Christian" tradition that wouldn't let me reach out.

I wish I could report that two decades later all that is behind us. But it's not. In 1976 religious fundamentalist Jimmy Carter campaigned in black churches all across this country, singing, "We shall overcome." Yet in his very own church, blacks were not welcome. So blind was he to the moral contradiction of a "racist Christian church" that it never even occurred to him that attending a segregated church might prove to be a political embarrassment.

As I spoke around the country after the 1976 elections I found white evangelicals eager to believe that Carter's church was an exception. But it was not an exception; it was the rule.

In 1978 my granddaughter was turned away from the day care center at Calvary Baptist Church just six blocks east of Voice of Calvary.

Two years ago several white Voice of Calvary volunteers from the Church of the Brethren in Pennsylvania attended a Bill Gothard seminar in Jackson. During one session, people from the all-white Parkway Baptist Church, six blocks west of VOC, invited them to their Christmas program. The volunteers invited Jean Thomas, a VOC staff member from Haiti, to go along with them. When the group showed up at the church, Jean was not allowed in the sanctuary.

I would say that today in Mississippi only one white city church in 10, and no more than one rural church in a hundred, would accept a black into membership.

Paul B. Henry comments:

> The blame and the remedy for our social evils [belongs] on the shoulders of the 40 million evangelicals in this country. If we can't solve the problem of racism in our own churches, what right do we have to pontificate to the rest of the world? If we can't

place our loyalty to the demands of God over and above our loyalty to the nation, how can we truly call ourselves soldiers of the Cross? And if we can't divest ourselves of our captivity to suburban, materialistic American culture, how can we speak to the maldistribution of wealth in our country and around the world?[3]

The evangelical church, with a few remarkable exceptions, remains the greatest stronghold of the sin of racism in America today.

What a tragic betrayal of the gospel of reconciliation!

REFLECTION

1. The author's faithfulness to the gospel demanded that he be both an evangelical and a civil rights advocate. Yet he quickly discovered that most evangelicals opposed the civil rights movement. In your opinion, why did the evangelical church "have no room for social justice"?
2. The author claims that the church is still the most racist institution in America, maintaining segregation long after racial barriers have fallen in other social institutions. How do you explain this fact when the gospel demands that the church lead the way in the work of reconciliation?
3. The author believes that the civil rights movement needed evangelical leaders, and that the evangelical church missed a tremendous opportunity when it failed to provide civil rights leadership during the sixties. How might the civil rights movement have been different if the evangelical church had led the way in sounding the call for justice and reconciliation?
4. Is the church's failure to provide leadership in the area of social justice an opportunity lost forever, or is there still opportunity?
5. Who are the oppressed in your community? What will it mean to bring liberty to these specific oppressed people? What can your church do to help bring release to the oppressed in your community? What can you do?

3

SHEEP WITHOUT
A SHEPHERD

One institution—and only one—held the key to change for black America.

We needed laws to protect our civil rights. Justice demanded it. But we couldn't wait on government to decide to act.

Schools needed to be improved. That was crucial to our education. But change wouldn't come from the schools.

The business community would have to change too. We needed equal employment opportunities, equal access to vocational training, equal access to business credit. Boycotts helped, but they weren't enough. And the business community wasn't going to initiate change.

Yes, the white man had put us into this predicament, but we could not expect him to get us out of it. And every one of these social institutions—the government, the school system, and the business community—was controlled by whites. If change was to come it would have to be led by blacks. Reverend Odenwald hit the nail on the head when he had said in effect, "I can't set them free, but you can."

Yes, whites could help. In fact, help from whites was a

must, whether through schools, government, business, or other institutions. But the responsibility to lead lay squarely on our shoulders. And in twentieth-century America, that meant that only one institution could be the vehicle for that change—the black church.

The black church, you see, was *ours*. Before the Civil War slave masters appointed white preachers to pastor their slaves, making the church just one more tool of domination. A favorite text was, "Slaves, obey your masters" (see Col. 3:22). But with the Emancipation, the number of black churches in the South mushroomed. At last we had one social institution that was ours. This newly independent church was the one place where we enjoyed true freedom of speech. It was the one place where, for a few hours a week, we could feel really free. So we often spent the whole day at church. Naturally, then, the black church came to be not only the center of spiritual life but also the focus of social life and culture for the religious and not-so-religious black alike.

Because the church provided the only setting where black leadership could arise, the preacher quickly became the central figure in the black community. It was to the church, then, that the black community turned for leadership. If change was to take place it would start there. The church, and only the church, held within its grasp the means to bring to fruition the hopes and dreams of black America.

Mendenhall was overrun with the very kinds of needs the church was so strategically positioned to meet. The people had become resigned to their plight; the church could inspire hope. The promising young people were leaving the community while only the unmotivated were staying; the church was in a position to train young leaders. The public schools were struggling to provide an adequate education; the church could create a tutoring program or a preschool. About the only recreational facilities for youth in Mendenhall were the honky-tonks; the church could plan wholesome youth activities.

That was just the beginning. Our people desperately needed better nutrition, housing, child care, employment, and more. Creative, visionary leadership from the church could mobilize the people to tackle each of these problems head on.

To bring true freedom, though, church leaders would not only have to be strong and creative, they would also have to be true to the gospel. They would have to stand not for some form of reactionary separatism but for reconciliation with our white brothers and sisters. Howard Snyder is right on target when he asserts:

> Reconciliation with God must be demonstrated by genuine reconciliation within the Christian community and by a continuing ministry of reconciliation in the world.
>
> This means that in each local Christian assembly reconciliation must be more than a theory and more than an invisible spiritual transaction. Reconciliation must be real and visible. Racial and economic exploitation and all forms of elitism . . . must be challenged biblically. Unholy divisions in the body of Christ must be seen as sin and worldliness (1 Cor. 3:3-4).[4]

A local church fellowship living out a gospel which burns through racial barriers could bring freedom to blacks and whites alike. With the Spirit's power and the wholehearted cooperation of the people, our faith could make Mendenhall a different place!

The church held the key—but it wasn't using it.

Even as I sat in Reverend Morris's study on that Sunday afternoon in 1961—shocked, hurt, rejected—I saw one thing more clearly than ever before: he didn't know his people. He didn't know their needs, their concerns, their hopes, their dreams. And he didn't know the needs of the community. How could he? With four other churches to pastor he was in town to preach only twice a month. And because he was seldom there, his leading the congregation in making Mendenhall a better place was totally out of the question.

I knew it wasn't just Reverend Morris. That's just the way the system worked. To be considered full-time, a preacher had to have at least four churches—one for each Sunday of the month. A preacher with five or six churches was considered outstanding. So the preacher would live in a town like Jackson or Hattiesburg and show up at each church once or twice a month to preach.

The people didn't really mind the preacher living out of town. In fact they liked it that way. They were afraid that if the preacher lived in town he might find out how they lived. Or they might see him make a mistake and lose confidence in him.

Even an immoral preacher could easily put on a religious front for Sunday services. It was easy for the congregation, too, to be religious one or two Sundays a month when the preacher was around. The whole system of absentee leadership encouraged both pastor and people to live a light, superficial Christianity which could challenge the morals of neither.

The preacher didn't see it as his job to know the needs of his people. He didn't see it as his job to know the needs of the community. He didn't see it as his job to lead his people in putting their faith to work in a way that would make a difference in their community.

What, then, was his role? In an environment of fear, hostility, and oppression, the church provided a release valve. Christianity was not seen as a force to change the situation, but as an emotional outlet to make it easier to endure. Black preachers had accepted this view of the church. Bible teaching, therefore, was considered secondary in most churches. What was important was "good preaching," and "good preaching" meant preaching that aroused the emotions and got people to shout.

But the church's failure went beyond lack of leadership. The church itself became the oppressor. Rather than working to free his people from poverty, the preacher often added to it by exploiting them. Dolphus Weary, now executive director of Mendenhall VOC, describes his early memories of his pastor:

> My own minister would come to our house during revival times. My mother would prepare food for him: meat, cakes, vegetables, anything. And we children had to wait and end up eating what was left over. She'd save up all her money and then he'd come in and eat up all the food. She'd pay her little bit of money in the church and he'd drive a big car while here we were living in a shack and sharing our money with him. Somehow this didn't jive in my mind.[5]

It was just as Peter predicted: "There will also be false teachers among you . . . and many will follow their sensuality, and because of them the way of the truth will be maligned; and in their greed they will exploit you with false words; their judgment from long ago is not idle, and their destruction is not asleep" (2 Pet. 2:1-3).

The situation is not much better today. While our cities cry out for help, many of our pastors gather to show off their expensive suits and impressive Cadillacs. America's blacks, with few exceptions, remain sheep without real shepherds. Ezekiel's prophecy speaks directly to our situation: "Then the word of the Lord came to me saying, 'Son of man, prophesy against the shepherds of Israel. Prophesy and say to those shepherds, "Thus says the Lord God, 'Woe, shepherds of Israel who have been feeding themselves! Should not the shepherds feed the flock? You eat the fat and clothe yourselves with the wool, you slaughter the fat sheep without feeding the flock. Those who are sickly you have not strengthened, the diseased you have not healed, the broken you have not bound up, the scattered you have not brought back, nor have you sought for the lost; but with force and with severity you have dominated them. And they were scattered for lack of a shepherd, and they became food for every beast of the field and were scattered. My flock wandered through all the mountains and on every high hill, and My flock was scattered over all the surface of the earth; and there was no one to search or seek for them.'"' Therefore, you shepherds, hear the word of the Lord: 'As I live,' declares the Lord God, 'surely because My flock has become a prey, My flock has even become food for all the beasts of the field for lack of a shepherd, and My shepherds did not search for My flock, but rather the shepherds fed themselves and did not feed My flock; therefore, you shepherds, hear the word of the Lord: "Thus says the Lord God, 'Behold, I am against the shepherds, and I shall demand My sheep from them and make them cease from feeding sheep. So the shepherds will not feed themselves any more, but I shall deliver My flock from their mouth, that they may not be food for them'"'" (Ezek. 34:1-10).

Our church then has failed—failed to provide the kind of leadership that can bring its people a deeper knowledge of

God, freedom from poverty and dependence, and a new sense of self-love.

You ask, What about Jesse Jackson? He's doing a great work. What about Tom Skinner? He's doing a great work. What about Reverend Leon Sullivan, Dr. Ruben Connors, Dr. E. V. Hill, Dr. Bill Pannell, and others?

Yes, there are a few preachers scattered across the country doing great work. My message is not directed to them. My message is directed to those shepherds who have not laid down their lives for their sheep, but have left them to wander.

In Cabrini Green on Chicago's near north side, where the mayor has had to move in to try to contend with crime, where blacks kill blacks, 14,000 people are wandering with few real shepherds. In Brooklyn, Harlem, Watts, and the south side of Chicago, sheep wander without shepherds. In Jackson, Mississippi, the Mississippi Delta and the ghettos of Philadelphia and Pittsburgh, sheep wander without shepherds. In our communities where people are hurting the worst, faithful, self-sacrificing shepherds are woefully scarce.

Our churches must come alive! I believe the only hope for the black community, yes, maybe the only hope for America, lies within the black church. The time has come for America's black pastors to provide the kind of creative leadership that today's crisis demands.

Twenty-eight percent of black families are poor. Robbery and rape are at epidemic proportions. Thirty percent of the girls showing up at the abortion clinics are black. Prostitution is at an all-time high. About 46 percent of all black families are single-parent households. The lack of a father image, especially for our young boys, is leading to rebellion and crime.

About 50 percent of our black children who enter the first grade drop out before they finish high school. Only 20 percent enter college, and less than eight percent graduate.

The shortage of decent housing grows more severe every day. In our cities crime infests the subsidized, high-rise apartments. Our elderly are being neglected in dilapidated old folks' homes.

To rise above these problems we must raise up a new generation of black leaders—men and women who love God and believe that the gospel has the power to bring salvation and liberation from sin. And we must define sin to include every wrong, corporate or individual, that threatens the dignity of man.

We must raise up leaders who will develop church fellowships that really know how to be the Body of Christ and to carry out His mission.

We must raise up leaders, filled with the Spirit of God, who will go back to our ghettos and depressed rural communities and administer healing. Leaders who will forego "the treasures of Egypt" for a season and choose rather to suffer affliction with our own people (see Heb. 11:26). Their leadership cannot be styled after the old leadership nor after the white suburban church; it must be uniquely designed to respond to the specific needs of a people trampled by society.

We must raise up leaders with the vision to set up counseling centers, drug rehabilitation centers, homes offering girls an alternative to abortion. We must go into our prisons and into our ghettos to proclaim hope to those who have lost all hope (see Luke 4:18).

As we embark on our mission, we must invite our white brothers and sisters to join us—to join us as partners in a way that reconciles us to each other even as we labor together. But if we extend the invitation and no one comes, we cannot wait to start. We must start without them.

Time is running out. We cannot wait. *We* must take the responsibility to save our people and our nation.

Real change will come only when our leaders, filled with the Spirit of God and armed with a holistic gospel, relocate within the community of need. We must live among our people, agonize with them, make their needs our needs. Then we must join with them in solving their problems with God's power.

We must truly shepherd our people—live among them, love them, lead them. That's what it's going to take to make a difference.

REFLECTION

1. Why does the author feel that the black church is so crucial to bringing positive change for black America?
2. In America, what has been the traditional role for the black preacher? How has this traditional approach to leadership hindered the development of spiritually healthy congregations?
3. The author believes that we must "raise up a new generation of black leaders." What kind of leaders does the black church need if it is to effectively minister to the total needs of America's blacks?

THE VISION
4. **Here Am I. Send Me!**
5. **I Have a Dream, Too**

4

HERE AM I.
SEND ME!

When a person starts to criticize the people doing a certain job, when he is forever trying to persuade someone else to do it, more than likely God is calling him to do that job himself. That was certainly true for me.

Our Mendenhall ministry was two years old. We were holding Sunday School, teaching Bible classes for youth and adults two nights a week, and conducting Youth for Christ rallies each Saturday night. Young people were learning about the Bible, growing in the Lord. And while many of them went to church the one Sunday each month the preacher came to town, that didn't satisfy them. They started coming to me and saying, "We want a church. We want a place where we can worship every Sunday and really learn about the Bible."

I knew that starting a church would unleash all the hostility of the other pastors in the area against us. They would see us as competition.

But the young people were right. I knew they were. We did need a church. God never intended for Christians to grow in isolation. He wanted us to grow within a fellowship of people living together as a Body. So we shared a growing yearning to become a fellowship.

But there was a problem—we had no preacher. Who would pastor the people? Who would give the sermons Sunday after Sunday? That wasn't my talent. I was a Bible teacher, a youth worker, not a pastor. So I was locked in a struggle. These young people were gathering around me, but they had no pastor. They were sheep without a shepherd.

Over the months, God's call became increasingly clear. He was calling me to move beyond criticizing the church for its failure; He was calling me to establish a church body. But I felt so inadequate. I felt as Isaiah felt when he moved into the presence of God and said, "Woe is me, for I am ruined! Because I am a man of unclean lips, And I live among a people of unclean lips; For my eyes have seen the King, the Lord of hosts" (Isa. 6:5).

Just as Isaiah had to settle it, I also had to settle it. He says in verse 8: "Then I heard the voice of the Lord, saying, 'Whom shall I send, and who will go for Us?' Then I said, 'Here am I. Send me!'"

That year the fellowship was on its way. I became the pastor. Because I felt so inadequate, from the beginning I asked other people to share in the preaching—Artis Fletcher, Dolphus Weary, Sister Andrus, and Leonard Stapleton. In the early days Joe Gene Walker came up from New Hebron to help sometimes. From the beginning the church was led not by one man, but by a team. To this day it is one of the few black churches in Mississippi with more than one full-time pastor.

God's call to pastor a church was only one of several calls God has made on my life. I could never have survived our years in Mendenhall without being sure God had called us to be there. There were times I wanted to leave, I wanted to bail out.

One of the first such times came just six months after we moved back to Mississippi. We were still living in New Hebron with Vera's grandmother. Grandma's house, to say the least, was not the healthiest environment imaginable. We were crowded, we had no running water and no nearby stream. Phillip, our third child, started running a fever and limping. A local doctor prescribed medicine to relieve him, but Phillip didn't get better; he only got worse. We wanted to take him to a specialist but we didn't have the money. We didn't know what to do.

Vera Mae began to get uneasy and started talking about going back to California. There I could have a good-paying job and we could afford medical care and a decent house and just possibly save Phillip's life.

Each morning during those days I got up and went out to our church where I would pray in a back room. I usually read Scripture before I prayed, but on one morning I felt that God was pressing me to make a decision. On the one hand I felt that God had called us here. On the other hand my son was suffering, getting worse and worse. In fact I had already picked out a grave site for him.

The pressure on me was tremendous. As I knelt there before the Lord the choice seemed clearcut—stay where God had called me and bury my son or go back to California and save his life.

As I picked up my Bible to read, it fell open to that passage where Peter said, "Behold, we have left everything and followed you." And Jesus said, "Truly I say to you, there is no one who has left house or brothers or sisters or mother or father or children or farms, for My sake and for the gospel's sake, but that he shall receive a hundred times as much now in the present age . . . and in the world to come, eternal life" (Mark 10:28-30).

My feelings were probably much the same as Abraham's had been when God asked him to give up Isaac. God's will or my son—that was my choice. And right there I settled it—I would stay. I got up, convinced God would take Phillip, but with a sense of peace, of release. I was going to do God's will. I went home and told Vera Mae, "I've given Phillip up to the Lord."

A few weeks later the Lord opened the way for us to take him to an excellent doctor in Louisiana who diagnosed his condition—polio.

The night we found out what was wrong with him, we got down on our knees and prayed, "God, please don't take him; raise him up." Later that summer we were able to take him to a special children's hospital in California. The doctors there confirmed the diagnosis but said that he had begun to heal. About a year later the same hospital gave him a clean bill of health. Phillip went on to be a football star at Jackson State

University. God's healing was complete!

There were other times I wanted to leave, too. Almost all the time, in fact. Why? I suppose it was mostly because I didn't feel accepted, especially after both the white church and black church in the area rejected me. But leaving would have meant turning my back on God's call. And getting out of God's call just isn't all that easy to do. Remember Moses? And Jonah?

I've run across a lot of fiery-eyed young people who declare, "God has called me to come here." Then two weeks later, when things get a little bit rough, they're on the bus headed back home. God's call doesn't work that way.

I believe the call of God is sort of a trap—He pushes us in and then closes the door. We can't just run in and out. God's call is when God nails your feet to the floor.

One proof that you're really called of God is that you can never get away from that call. I've met men in old folks' homes who tell me that years before God called them with a message, but they didn't carry the message. They are some of the saddest old men I've ever met. You can say no to God's call, but you can never be at peace without obeying it.

I even think that you can listen for the voice of God the second time. It seems that God had clearly called Abraham to separate himself from his family but Abraham took his father and his family with him to Haran and lived there for five years until his father died. Only then did Abraham finally leave and go to Canaan. It seems like he remembered or he heard the voice of God the second time. God called him five years earlier. He went half the way then stopped and delayed. But he couldn't escape the call (see Gen. 12,13).

We too are tempted to follow God's will halfway, to see God's blessings then to live within the shadow of those blessings. It was not until Abraham fully obeyed God's call by separating himself from Lot, his last family member, that he fully experienced the blessings of God.

Jonah clearly heard God calling him to go to Nineveh, yet went down to Joppa and boarded a ship sailing for Tarshish. But even in the belly of the fish he recognized that he was wrestling with God. When he got out of the fish, the Bible says, "The word of the Lord came to Jonah the second time, saying, 'Arise, go to Nineveh the great city' " (Jon. 3:1,2).

That seems to be a pattern that runs throughout the Scriptures. Many of those whom God called, heard His call after a second time. So God's call is not easily escaped. It is clear. God makes the vision plain. He does not give a fuzzy picture.

Unless you have heard that call, don't go! After Absalom was killed, Joab sent a Cushite to David with news of the battle. Another runner named Ahimaaz wanted to carry the message. He kept begging Joab to let him go until Joab finally let him run. Ahimaaz outran the Cushite and got to David first with the news of victory. But when David asked, "Is it well with the young man Absalom?" Ahimaaz had to answer, "I saw a great tumult, but I did not know what it was" (2 Sam. 18:29). Then the Cushite came and delivered the news. Ahimaaz had run without being sent. He had run without having the message, so David didn't hear the news from him.

So if you haven't heard the message, if you haven't heard that call, don't go! Don't move, don't run, don't go into the community, don't go into the ghetto, don't go anywhere unless you have a clear call of God. But if you have heard God's call, run!

When God calls, He calls us to a hazardous mission. God commanded Isaiah: "Go, and tell this people: 'Keep on listening, but do not perceive; keep on looking, but do not understand.' Render the hearts of this people insensitive, their ears dull, and their eyes dim, lest they see with their eyes, hear with their ears, understand with their hearts, and repent and be healed" (Isa. 6:9,10).

When God calls He doesn't invite us to a picnic. He calls us to go to a stiff-necked, rebellious, stubborn people. Our success is not measured by fame; it is not measured by popularity contests; it is not measured by how many people raise their hands; it is not measured by how many souls were won today. God doesn't call us to that kind of task. Rather, God calls us to faithfulness. "Be faithful until death, and I will give you the crown of life" (Rev. 2:10). That's the key—faithfulness to God's call.

God calls us; He locks us in; but He never leaves us alone. He goes with us. He sustains us. That is the only assurance we have.

You know, if you think you're going to sink you panic. Ever since God first called me I have lived on the verge of panic. I've always been in over my head. I've always been doing things I knew I couldn't do. I've been like Peter walking on the water—always on the verge of sinking because he was doing something that took more power than he had. If he took his eyes off of Jesus—off of God's power—and looked at the storm he would sink.

Obeying God's call is like that. God never calls us to do something we can do in our own strength. He always calls us to get in over our heads—to move out to where we'll have to either depend on His power, or sink. Jackie Robinson put it this way: "I never had it made." Jackie always got in over his head. The person who follows God never has it made.

My first year back in Mississippi I found myself in the public schools. Here I was, a third grade dropout, didn't know a verb from anything else, and I was lecturing every week in front of all these educated teachers. I was in over my head.

And now when I'm sitting in the Senate dining hall with Senator Hatfield, or when I'm sitting on the platform with Billy Graham, or when I'm speaking at a convention with someone like Tom Skinner or Chuck Colson, I always realize I'm out of my league. I can only justify being there in one way—God called me. God picked up an ignorant guy like me, saved me, and pushed me into His ministry. I have no business doing what I'm doing except that God called me to do it.

People often say to me, "John, you're successful. You've done it." But I've never quite arrived. And just whenever I think I'm about to arrive, God leads me somewhere else. And it is always to do something that I'm not up to.

At this very moment, at the age of 52, I am hearing a new call. God is saying, "John Perkins, I want you to go out again, just like you did when I called you back to Mississippi 22 years ago." The exact shape of this call isn't yet clear to me. But one thing is clear: God is calling me to serve those communities where my people are trapped in sin and oppression. Where a sense of inferiority breeds crime, hopelessness, and self-destruction.

I realize that only Christ living in those communities can save my people. And it is up to us to bring Him alive there.

God will do very little apart from His people.

You too can know where God is calling you to serve. You can know what He is calling you to do. How?

First, test your understanding of God's call with Scripture. God's Word will always confirm His call. He never calls us to do anything that contradicts the Word. For example, God will never call a Christian to marry an unbeliever, for His Word says, "Do not be bound together with unbelievers" (2 Cor. 6:14).

Second, share your call with Christians whom you trust for counsel so they can affirm what God is saying to you. One of these persons should be a pastor.

Third, watch for a sense of relief and contentment to come as you take the first steps of obedient response to that call. It will come if God has truly called you.

Finally, after embarking on this ministry, listen for God's voice for further direction. Not until you are totally submerged in God's will should you expect His full plan to be revealed to you.

That is where we were in Mendenhall. God had called us; we were sure of that. We had answered His call. He had given us a knowledge of the needs of the people, a vision for what needed to be done. But He hadn't yet shown us a strategy for doing it.

I had heard the voice of God saying, "Whom shall I send, and who will go for Us?"

And I had answered, "Here am I. Send me!" (Isa. 6:8).

REFLECTION

1. This chapter opens: "When a person starts to criticize the people doing a certain job, when he is forever trying to persuade someone else to do it, more than likely God is calling him to do that job himself." Can you think of a time when this was true of you?
2. Why is it dangerous to go without being sent?
3. At the end of the chapter the author suggests four guidelines for recognizing God's call. How have you been able to recognize God's call in your own life?

5

I HAVE A DREAM, TOO

August 26, 1963. The drama unfolded against the backdrop of the Lincoln Memorial. Television cameras, broadcasting the historic event into millions of living rooms and offices throughout the nation, panned the expectant throng, over 200,000 strong. The occasion—the march on Washington.

The sun beat down and the afternoon wore on as a parade of speakers and singers issued impassioned pleas for liberty and justice for all.

Then A. Philip Randolph, the march organizer, introduced the day's final speaker: ". . . a philosopher of the nonviolent system of behavior, in seeking to bring about social change for the advancement of justice and freedom and dignity—I have the pleasure to present to you Dr. Martin Luther King!"

The crowd erupted into a cheering, applauding, chanting, banner-waving mass of humanity. Dr. King had to wait a long minute before he could be heard above the crowd.

Then his voice rang out with the now-famous words of this speech, "I Have a Dream," in which he proclaimed in part:

> Five score years ago, a great American, in whose symbolic shadow we stand, signed the Emancipation Proclamation.

. . . But one hundred years later, we must face the tragic fact that the Negro is still not free. One hundred years later, the life of the Negro is still sadly crippled by the manacles of segregation and the chains of discrimination. One hundred years later, the Negro lives on a lonely island of poverty in the midst of a vast ocean of material prosperity.

. . . There are those who are asking the devotees of civil rights, "When will you be satisfied?" We can never be satisfied as long as the Negro is the victim of unspeakable horrors of police brutality. We can never be satisfied as long as our bodies, heavy with the fatigue of travel, cannot gain lodging in the motels of the highways and the hotels of the cities. We cannot be satisfied as long as the Negro's basic mobility is from a smaller ghetto to a larger one. We can never be satisfied as long as a Negro in Mississippi cannot vote and a Negro in New York believes he has nothing for which to vote. No, no, we are not satisfied, and we will not be satisfied until justice rolls down like waters and righteousness like a mighty stream.

. . . I say to you today, my friends, that in spite of the difficulties and frustrations of the moment, I still have a dream. It is a dream deeply rooted in the American dream.

I have a dream that one day this nation will rise up and live out the true meaning of its creed: "We hold these truths to be self-evident; that all men are created equal."

I have a dream that one day on the red hills of Georgia the sons of former slaves and the sons of former slaveowners will be able to sit down together at the table of brotherhood.

I have a dream that one day even the state of Mississippi, a desert state, sweltering with the heat of injustice and oppression, will be transformed into an oasis of freedom and justice.

I have a dream that my four little children will one day live in a nation where they will not be judged by the color of their skin but by the content of their character.

. . . This will be the day when all of God's children will be able to sing with new meaning, "My country, 'tis of thee, sweet land of liberty, of thee I sing. Land where my fathers died, land of the pilgrim's pride, from every mountainside, let freedom ring."

. . . When we let freedom ring, when we let it ring from every village and every hamlet, from every state and every city, we will be able to speed up that day when all of God's children, black men and white men, Jews and Gentiles, Protestants and Catholics, will be able to join hands and sing in the words of the old Negro spiritual, "Free at last! free at last! thank God Almighty, we are free at last!"[6]

In those words, Martin Luther King captured many of my own hopes and dreams. His dream was my dream too. Yet at that very time God was at work in my heart, shaping a dream bigger than the American dream, a dream rooted in the very gospel of Jesus Christ.

As our little congregation in Mendenhall took shape my faith was approaching a crucial test. Mechanization was displacing Mississippi sharecroppers, driving them even deeper into poverty. Racial tensions were rising. The problems plaguing our little community were so great, and we were so few. What could we do?

Did the gospel have the power to tear down evil traditions and institutions? Was there a faith stronger than culture? A faith that could burn through racial, cultural, economic and social barriers?

I remember as if it were yesterday how I started searching the Scriptures for principles, for a strategy I could follow. God's answer came one day as I read the story of the woman at the well in John 4.

First, I noticed how Jesus approached the woman. *He came to her on her territory.* He *chose* to go through Samaria. Jews traveling from Judea to Galilee usually crossed over the Jordan River and went around Samaria because of their prejudice. A Jew meeting a Samaritan on the road would cross to the other side to keep even the shadow of the Samaritan from touching him. Jesus deliberately went through Samaria for one reason—He wanted to personally touch the lives of the people there.

Second, the Holy Spirit showed me this profound truth: *Jesus' love, His bodily presence in a community, could reconcile people.* A ray of hope appeared. Jesus had gone to Samaria and evangelized the Samaritans. He had burned through racial barriers! Here was a method we could use! If Jesus' bodily presence had overcome racial barriers in Samaria, His presence in Mendenhall as His Body could burn through racial barriers here. We, the church, were His Body. Through us, as us, He was just as present in our community as He had been that day in Samaria. Here was the key to reconciliation! The reconciliation *we* were powerless to bring, Christ could bring supernaturally through the presence of His Body, through His people, the church!

Third, I saw how Jesus opened the conversation with the woman. *He let her felt need determine the starting point of the conversation.* She was at the well to get water; He asked for a drink. Notice that He didn't just talk about *her* need; He brought His own need. Her need was water; His need was water. And by asking her to give, by asking her to help Him, He affirmed her dignity. Man's most deeply felt need is to have his dignity affirmed. He wants to feel his somebody-ness—to know that he is a person of worth. That is what the woman at the well needed to know. She needed to know that she was as good as a Jew.

Jesus not only affirmed the woman's dignity, He also empowered her to rise above her past. He offered her living water which would free her from her self-destructive life-style. So while He met her at the point of her felt need, He did not stop there. That felt need became the stepping-stone to His meeting her deeper need.

When we meet people at the point of their felt needs we avoid the trap of arbitrarily defining their problems for them and imposing our "solutions" on them. If we respond to their felt needs not with a dependency-producing charity, but rather with identification with the need, with receiving as well as giving and with an empowering response that permanently lifts them above their past, then we help them to become all God has in mind for them to be. This "felt-need concept" would prove to be foundational to our ministry strategy.

From this story I had gotten my first glimpse of three principles.

1. Jesus went *into* Samaria. He was physically present in the community of need. He met the woman at the point of her need as she perceived it. He identified with her felt need.

2. Jesus' love, His bodily presence in the community, burned through racial barriers, reconciling Jew and Samaritan. In the same way the presence of Christ's Body in a community today could bring people together.

3. Finally, Jesus related to the woman in a way that invited her to give to Him; He did not simply give to her. In doing this He affirmed her dignity. Then by offering her living water He related to her in a way that empowered her to rise above her past.

Within these principles lay the seed of a strategy for the church, a strategy we would come to call the three *R's* of Christian community development.

The first *R* is *relocation.* To minister effectively to the poor I must relocate in the community of need. By living as a neighbor with the poor, the needs of the community become my own. I am no longer isolated in a suburban community. Shared needs and friendships become a bridge for communicating the good news of Jesus Christ and working together for better conditions in the community.

If we are going to be the Body of Christ, shouldn't we do as He did? He didn't commute daily from heaven to earth to minister to us. Nor did He set up a mission compound which would make Him immune to our problems. No, He became flesh and lived among us (see John 1:14).

The second *R* is *reconciliation.* The gospel has the power to reconcile people both to God and to each other. Man's reconciliation to God through Jesus Christ is clearly the heart of the gospel. But we must also be reconciled to each other. Reconciliation across racial, cultural, and economic barriers is not an optional aspect of the gospel. I need you and you need me, and we need each other. God commands us to love and forgive one another. Our love for one another demonstrates to the world that we are indeed Jesus' disciples (see John 13:35). I must be reconciled to both God and man.

The third *R* is *redistribution*. Christ calls us to share with those in need. This calls for redistributing more than our goods. It means sharing our skills, our time, our energy, and our gospel in ways that empower people to break out of the cycle of poverty and assume responsibility for their own needs. We must organize business enterprises within the community of need which will be owned by a broad base of people. This will mean using such methods as cooperatives, mutual savings and loan associations, and credit unions. The goal of redistribution is not absolute equality, but a more equitable distribution of resources.

After Jesus' disciples returned to the well, Jesus looked up and saw the Samaritans coming out to Him from the city. To His disciples He said, "Do you not say, 'There are yet four months, and then comes the harvest?' Behold, I say to you, lift up your eyes, and look on the fields, that they are white for harvest" (John 4:35).

The fields of America are also white, ready for harvest. The needs will not wait. The problems will not go away.

According to recent Gallup polls, 40 million Americans profess to be "born again" and believe that the Bible is infallibly inspired. The same polls, however, reveal that crime and immorality in America are rising to unprecedented levels. Religion is up and morality is down. Despite its growth, the church is not bringing healing to our nation. It is not penetrating our communities with a message that transforms.

Conditions in the black community are especially bleak. Though blacks make up only 11 percent of the population—

- 70 percent of the U.S. prison population is black;
- in major American cities, 50 percent of all black children are born out of wedlock;
- 46 percent of black families are single-parent families;
- in 1977 more blacks were killed by other blacks than were killed in the entire nine years of the Vietnamese conflict (*Ebony*, August 1979);
- the National Alliance for Family Life reports that half of all blacks getting married this year will be divorced within two years.

In light of these figures, the need for evangelism is critical. Our day calls for an evangelism that touches people where they live—one that speaks to their felt needs. Our day calls for a gospel that reconciles black and white, for unless we preach a gospel of reconciliation we preach no gospel at all.

In the face of such spiritual and human need the church's flight to the suburbs cannot go unchallenged. How can we claim to be loyal to Christ's mission when we flee the mission field at our doorstep? When we forsake the inner city so that our lives will not be inconvenienced by the sufferings of the neediest among us? We flee the very mission fields we should be invading. We try to soothe our consciences with such token ministries to the poor as tracts and media—nice, safe "ministries" that do not require living or working among the poor, "ministries" that insulate us from sharing in their suffering.

The poor of America today are at the mercy of politicians' whims and philanthropists' charity. Neither politicians nor philanthropists can offer people what they need the most—the incarnate love of Christ. Unless the church fulfills its responsibility to proclaim by word and deed the "Good News to the poor," the poor have no true hope. We, the church, bear the only true gospel of hope. Only through us can the power of Christ's love save and deliver them. *The fate of America's poor is in our hands.*

My dream is to see healing come to our nation through the power of the gospel with a strategy of relocation, reconciliation, and redistribution. "The harvest is plentiful, but the workers are few. Therefore beseech the Lord of the harvest to send out workers into His harvest" (Matt. 9:37,38).

That is my dream.

REFLECTION

1. Review the excerpts of Dr. King's "I Have a Dream" speech. How consistent with Scripture do you believe Dr. King's dream was?
2. What does the author mean by the "felt need concept"? Give an example of how it might work.
3. What are the three *Rs* of Christian community development? Briefly explain each one.
4. In what ways did the author's God-given dream go beyond the American dream in which Dr. King's speech was rooted?

THE STRATEGY

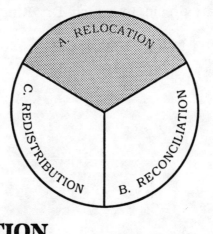

RELOCATION

6

YOUR NEED IS MY NEED

When we first moved back to Mississippi, the people were surprised and puzzled.

On the one hand they were glad to see us, happy we were back. At the same time they weren't at all sure we should be there. Nobody ever came back to Mississippi to live, especially after making it somewhere else. But there we were, June 9, 1960, in New Hebron, Mississippi, with our car, our trailer, and our kids. As far as people could tell, we had no income and no prospect of income. How could a preacher expect to make a living without pastoring some big church?

The seven of us moved into a little three-bedroom house with Vera Mae's grandmother. Christian friends in California had pledged to send $75 to $100 a month, but that certainly wouldn't feed a family of seven. So right away I started to work, cutting wood and picking cotton. At first, people were embarrassed that I was having to do this kind of work alongside them.

Though I didn't realize it at the time, those experiences were building the foundation for our ministry. The people were seeing that I really was one of them. I was not an outsider. I was not a "have" giving handouts to "have nots." I had given up a good job, a big comfortable house, and the freedom and respect I had enjoyed in California to return to the poverty, discomfort, and oppression I had left behind 13 years earlier. I was choosing to become a "have not" in order to take my people the gospel. I was once again becoming one of them. To reach my people I was following the same pattern Jesus had used to reach me. "For you know the grace of our Lord Jesus Christ, that though He was rich, yet for your sake He became poor, that you through His poverty might become rich" (2 Cor. 8:9).

James Cone describes this principle of love expressed through voluntary oppression in this way:

> The Christian community, therefore, is that community that freely becomes oppressed, because they know that Christ himself has defined humanity's liberation in the context of what happens to the little ones. Christians join the cause of the oppressed in the fight for justice not because of some philosophical principle of "the Good" or because of a religious feeling of sympathy for people in prison. Sympathy does not change the structures of injustice. The authentic identity of Christians with the poor is found in the claim which the Christ-encounter lays upon their own life-style, a claim that connects the word "Christian" with the liberation of the poor. Christians fight not for humanity in general but for themselves and out of their love for concrete human beings.[7]

Moses stands as a powerful example of this strategy because "he chose to be mistreated along with the people of God rather than to enjoy the pleasures of sin for a short time. He regarded disgrace for the sake of Christ as of greater value than the treasures of Egypt, because he was looking ahead to his reward" (Heb. 11:25-26, *NIV*).

In once again living among our people, their needs became our needs. Our shared needs, then, became the starting point of our ministry.

First of all, our needs opened the door for ministry by enabling the people to accept us as a part of them. Once they got over the embarrassment, we could minister to them in those cotton fields. The people knew that we really understood their problems, their needs, their feelings, because we had the same problems, the same needs, the same feelings. One reason God became flesh was so we would know that "we do not have a high priest who cannot sympathize with our weaknesses, but one who has been tempted in all things as we are" (Heb. 4:15). Now, God didn't have to become man to find out what our needs were; but we needed Him to become man so that we would know He knew our needs. Because He became one of us, we could be sure He understood.

Second, our needs opened the door for our ministry by putting us in a position to receive. Even in the area of food, their needs became our needs. People gave us milk, eggs, pecans, syrup. They raised hogs or cows for us. Every Christmas for nine years, Mrs. Owens from Calvary Bible Church in Burbank, California sent big boxes of new clothes and toys. At Mendenhall, folks let us pick beans or peas from their fields. Kids from the Bible classes helped us can or freeze them. We canned so many we couldn't eat them all.

We learned that making the needs of the poor our own didn't mean our needs would go unmet. *God always provided.* He always supplied all our "needs according to His riches in glory in Christ Jesus" (Phil. 4:9). And out of our receiving from others as well as sharing with them grew a strong sense of interdependence and community.

Third, the needs we shared with the community determined the shape of our ministry. We didn't come back to Mississippi with preconceived ideas of what programs we would start. Rather, our programs grew out of the needs we found there. We lived among the people, we knew their needs, we felt their needs—in fact, we shared their needs. They were our needs too. So, long before I discovered the "felt need concept" in Scripture, we were already living it.

The people in Mendenhall were hungry for good, solid Bible teaching because the churches offered so little of it. So right off we started Bible classes, our first ministry. Three years later when we built our church educational unit these classes expanded into a Bible Institute. We held classes every Tuesday and Thursday night for young people and adults. White pastors like Reverend Kenneth Noyes, a mission worker, and Dr. James Spencer, a Presbyterian pastor, taught at the institute until pressure from whites at the peak of the civil rights movement forced them to quit. Mrs. Annie Bell Harper, the founder of a local black high school, and Sister Lou Ella Andrus taught there too.

Through these Bible classes we discovered that many of our young people could not read, and some of the adults could not even fill out job applications. So we began offering remedial reading through the institute. The "felt need concept" was at work.

Our first social action program was our day-care center. My wife had her hands full with our own—six by now—so she had a wonderful young lady named Almeda helping her with our children. Vera Mae saw that she wasn't the only person in town needing help. A lot of the older kids were missing school to watch younger brothers and sisters while their parents worked. Once they had fallen a year or two behind in school, they were embarrassed to go back and be in a class with younger kids, so they just dropped out for good. Another problem was that while these teenage girls were baby-sitting, boys would visit and the girls would get pregnant.

Still another need was nutrition. Many of these children were eating so poorly that they were becoming mentally retarded.

Our day-care center, then, grew out of these needs. At first we had no educational purpose except to teach the children about Jesus. Our main goals were to feed each child a good meal each day and to get the older girls back into school so they could break out of the poverty cycle.

In 1966 our day-care center became a Head Start program which involved about 100 children and provided about 20 jobs in the community. Today we have our own preschool called Genesis One.

Every ministry of the Voice of Calvary has come about the same way—in response to the felt needs of the community. We started a tutoring program to supplement the inadequate education our kids were getting. We helped lead the voter registration drive in Simpson County as a response to the need for justice. Housing needs prompted us to form a housing co-op to build duplexes with FHA loans and rent them at low rates.

We built a playground and then a gym to meet the recreational needs of the youth. To combat poor nutrition we expanded our feeding program and started a cooperative food store. Eventually we developed a cooperative farm to raise fresh produce.

While Vera Mae was conducting a government-sponsored study of poverty in the community in 1969, we found a tremendous need for health care. The clinics that did exist all had separate waiting rooms for blacks and whites and rarely treated a black before the white waiting room was empty. Our first health center opened in 1973 in Mendenhall. We have since opened health centers in Jackson, New Hebron, and Jayess.

In 1973 we also started an adult education program offering reading, writing, typing, welding, and carpentry. In 1975 we opened our first thrift store in Mendenhall to sell recycled clothing and household items. We have since opened two thrift stores in Jackson and one in Edwards.

As we have responded to all these felt needs, God has given us an abundant spiritual harvest. For hand in hand with our social action, our economic development, and our work for justice, has gone the work of evangelism. Through tent meetings, Bible classes, Sunday School, school chapel programs, Child Evangelism Fellowship, and more, we have proclaimed the Good News. Everything else we have done has grown out of this gospel we preach.

This is the way it had to be. "A natural man does not accept the things of the Spirit of God; for they are foolishness to him, and he cannot understand them, because they are spiritually appraised" (1 Cor. 2:14). The natural man is more aware of his natural needs, not his spiritual needs, so that is where we had to meet him.

As we adopted Jesus' strategy of addressing people's felt needs, we had the chance to point to their deeper needs—their spiritual needs. As people saw our commitment to them, they began to look for the motivation behind our actions. We were then able to tell them about the love of Christ which compelled us to give our lives to serving them.

So we found that Jesus' felt-need strategy did work in Mendenhall. Again and again, touching people's felt needs opened the door to God's meeting their spiritual needs.

A strong healthy fellowship of believers grew up in Mendenhall. Since then another strong fellowship has grown up in Jackson. With VOC's help a new church in Canton has been planted, and now yet another fellowship is being formed in New Hebron.

Our approaches to the problems of the community have been far different from most of those traditionally taken by the government and other outside groups. Fortunately, some well-conceived government programs have been available to help us with community-based development. A depressed community striving to become self-sufficient needs outside technology and funds to get started. Government and other outside groups can provide these. But the programs themselves must be designed and led by the people of the community.

Voice of Calvary has been privileged to work with a growing number of government leaders who share our vision for community development. These include George A. Reich, M.D., Regional Health Administrator, Region IV, Atlanta, and his associates, Stephen H. King, M.D., Director of Health Services Division; Mr. Joseph E. Coon, Deputy Director of Health Services Division; and Ms. Irene Dunne, Project Officer. Our own governor William Winters and our state health officer, Alton Cobb, M.D., have been most supportive. Government can play an important role in community development, but it should neither design nor administer programs for the local community. That can only be done effectively by those actually living among the people.

Without relocation, without living among the people, without actually becoming one of the people, it is impossible to accurately identify the needs as the people perceive them. And once outsiders misdiagnose the problem, their proposed solutions cannot help but miss the mark. They will almost always treat symptoms without touching the disease. In fact, the relief of the uncomfortable symptoms may remove the incentive to cure the disease. The person in need becomes addicted to the program that provides temporary relief while the disease eats away at his humanity. The very program designed to save the victim destroys him.

This is why relocation, the first of the three *Rs*, is so important. An outsider can seldom know the needs of the community well enough to know how to best respond to them. Rarely if ever can an outsider effectively lead the community in finding creative solutions to its own problems. That kind of leadership, the kind of leadership that empowers people, comes from insiders.

That was the kind of leadership God was calling and enabling our fellowship to provide. God in the flesh, as His Body, had come to Mendenhall just as He had once gone to a little village in Samaria. Now as then, because of His presence, people's lives would never be the same.

REFLECTION

1. Have you ever moved to a new area and suddenly found you had some new needs simply because you were in a new neighborhood? What were some of those new needs?
2. Why is it important to live among the people you are ministering to?
3. How has identifying with the *felt needs* of others led to new ministries in your church? In your own life? Have these ministries ever led to opportunities to minister to people's deeper spiritual needs? If so, how?
4. What are some dangers of trying to minister to people without living among them? Can you give any examples?

FILLING THE
LEADERSHIP VACUUM

"I was pumping gas at a gas station in Mendenhall. It was just a job. There was no future in it. I was 23 years old, just out of the service, and had no idea, no vision for what I would do in the future."

Herbert Jones's testimony was not untypical. For a black young person in Mendenhall, the future held little hope. Yet with young people like Herbert rested the community's best hope.

You see, the black community in Mendenhall had few real leaders, few people with the vision and the skills to make a difference. The one institution with the potential to give leadership—the church—had left the driver's seat empty. The older blacks in Mendenhall lacked the necessary leadership skills. So that left the young. Our best hope was to develop new leaders from among the young.

Mendenhall had no shortage of promising young people. The most promising, though, went off to college and few came back. They were the kind of highly motivated kids that the big corporations wanted to hire. So why should they come back? What was there to come back to?

All the jobs in Simpson County, with the single exception of being a black preacher, were controlled by whites. So the only way blacks could work in Simpson County was to accommodate themselves to the racism of whites. This had a predictable result—blacks left in droves. Between 1960 and 1970, 2,210 more blacks left Simpson County than moved in—and that in a county whose 1970 black population was only 6,258. It was no small problem.

I saw what we had to do. First, we had to keep the kids in school until they graduated. Second, some of these young people had to go to college to be trained—outside of Mississippi where they could get a new vision. Third, some of them had to bring their skills back to Mendenhall to provide the needed leadership. This, I knew, would be the hardest of all.

My job in Mendenhall would not be finished until we raised up trained Christian leaders to take over my place in the ministry. How we would do that, I didn't know. But I made it my goal.

One Sunday we were coming back into Mendenhall after preaching. Our kids were sleeping in the station wagon. I had been telling Vera Mae how God had been dealing with me about developing leaders who would go away to get training, then come back to the community to lead in the ministry.

Vera Mae's response really haunted me: "I'll never have another house again," she said. "I just gave my life away—to nothing."

That really hurt. I can't stand someone who doesn't care for his own kids. And Vera Mae was saying that I had dragged her into a situation that was more sacrifice for her and the kids than she had ever been willing to make. We had given up a 12-room house in California only to struggle through nine months in New Hebron, and now we were cramped into a little rented house in Mendenhall.

As I shared with her my dream for leadership development, it hit her like a ton of bricks—she would be stuck here for the next 10 or 12 years! That's how long it would take to raise up leaders to replace us in the ministry. But as much as Vera's words hurt, I knew I had to stay. God had called me.

One of my toughest jobs in developing leaders was going to be showing these young people that they could make a differ-

ence. They had grown up in an environment that barraged
them with the same message every day: "You are inferior, powerless, and there's nothing you can do to change it." Every day
separate waiting rooms, separate water fountains, and a host
of other ever-present reminders repeated, "You're inferior.
You're nobody."

Somehow I had to help these kids discover their humanity.
I had to help them find a sense of dignity. I had to tap their
sense of somebody-ness. Only then would they be able to
believe they could make a difference.

I thought back to when I was a boy.

There was Mrs. Mabelle Armstrong. She had taught me
about black people in history like Frederick Douglas and
Booker T. Washington. She had taught me to love our people.
Then there was my grandmother, Aunt Babe Perkins. She had
taught me to love old people. Then when Christ came into my
life, Mr. Wayne Leitch started teaching me the Bible, and he
showed me that I needed to love everyone. I could see that God
had loved me and reached down and picked me up. And here
was this white Bible teacher taking all this time with me. That
said something powerful to me about God's love.

And then there were people like John McGill, Ed Anthony,
Dave Peacock, James Howard, Curry Brown, Pastor Richard-
son, Jim Winston, George Moore, Momma Wilson—they all
helped me grow. Then when I first came back to New Hebron,
Brother Isaac Newsom invited me to review the Sunday School
lesson in his class every Sunday morning. That had helped me
grow. Leadership, I was beginning to see, was not created in a
vacuum. God had used all these people to prepare me for leadership.

Now God was telling me to put 2 Timothy 2:2 into practice:
"And the things which you have heard from me in the presence of many witnesses, these entrust to faithful men, who
will be able to teach others also." I had been taught; now I was
to teach others in such a way that they could eventually
become leaders and teach still others.

So I started spending time with young men. There was
Artis Fletcher who lived across the street from our mission. I
got him to start working with me. I got Dolphus Weary to work
with me. Then there was Leonard Stapleton, a young barber. I

would spend hours and hours with him. And then there was big Herbert Jones—6′4″, 230 pounds. Here's his story:

One day Mrs. Perkins pulled up to my pump for some gas. She introduced herself, then asked, "Are you a Christian?"

Now I went to church and tried to do all the right things and all so I said, "Yeah, sure, I'm a Christian." I really thought I was.

Well, she invited me to the Youth for Christ meetings they were having, and I said I'd come. I didn't go that Saturday night. During the week, though, Reverend Perkins came by and invited me. So I decided to go. That night, in that tin storefront they called the Fisherman's Mission, I saw a lot of the young people I knew. I met Leonard Stapleton, one of the guys I really respected, and heard him tell in a plain way what it meant to have Jesus Christ living inside of him. That hit me hard.

Then Reverend Perkins got up to give a little message. I still remember it. He talked about, "What Is Success?" He spoke from the book of Daniel, how God made Daniel what he was. He said, "Success isn't something you wear, like clothes or a car; success is something you are. Jesus Christ can make you a success. He can make you a son of God, and you can work for Him."

That made sense to me. I didn't have any direction or guidance, and here was a chance to get some from God. I listened to the invitation to receive Christ, but I didn't go forward that night. I was under conviction and tempted to leave. Finally, the meeting ended. I got in my car, feeling like I was going to bust inside. I drove like crazy to get home, hoping I wouldn't get in a wreck or get killed before I had a chance to get right with God. When I got home, I got down beside my bed and asked Christ to come into my life.

Well, I started spending time with Herbert, too. I remember when Herbert drove a hog truck, I would get up at 5:00 in the morning, drive with him to load up those hogs, then go with

him to the Jackson Packing Company slaughter house. At
night Herbert would wash up that old hog truck and pick up
young people to bring to our tent meeting. Three or four
months after Herbert committed his life to Christ, he started
working for VOC part-time. So Herbert and I worked side by
side, digging, driving nails, doing whatever needed doing.
Herbert's home situation was bad so when we got our educational building finished, Herbert moved into a little room in
the back of it. He really began to grow in the Lord. Herbert had
an extra special gift with kids. Wherever he went he attracted
kids like a magnet. He became like a second father to my own
children.

Herbert was becoming a leader.

From early on this goal of developing leaders guided our
planning. We knew that for young people to grow to be leaders
they would have to stay in school. A big reason for starting a
day-care center was to get young people back into school.
Then to help them stay in school we created our tutoring program.

Well, within a few years we had gotten several of these kids
through high school and off to college. But then we ran into a
snag. When they came back for the summer there were no
jobs. So they started getting summer jobs in the big cities. I
began to wonder, "How on earth could we bring these young
people back to the community?"

It was the summer of 1968. Dolphus had come back to
spend the summer. Artis and Leonard were going to school at
Washington Bible College in Washington, D.C. and had jobs
up there. They had found a job for Dolphus too. So when
Dolphus got back from California he had three options: (1)
stay home and do nothing; (2) go back to California; or (3)
take that job in Washington.

I remember meeting with him and saying, "Dolphus, why
don't you ask the Lord for a job here with us—and then ask
Him to supply the money?"

That summer Dolphus took my little red Volkswagen and
got several volunteers to go with him to hold vacation Bible
schools all over that area. Before the summer was out, God
had provided the whole $3,000 we needed for the program.
Every summer after that, Dolphus came back to Mississippi to

work with other young people in vacation Bible schools and in the tutoring program.

From then on we provided summer jobs to bring our college students back to the community. These jobs gave our students two important opportunities. First, they put them in positions of responsibility where they could develop leadership skills. Second, as they worked among the people they began to see the needs of the people through their own eyes and to become burdened for the people.

About this time we started our Summer Enrichment Program. Even though our college students had been top students in high school in Mississippi they were having a tough time making Cs in out-of-state colleges. They would be expected to read a book in a day or two when they had never in their lives even read a whole book through. So we created the Summer Enrichment Program to help get our high school students ready for college.

To get at the dropout problem we later added a tutoring program. Upper-grade tutors earned $50.00 a week. Half of that went into savings for college or trade school and they got the other half to spend. Younger tutors received $30.00 a week, half of which went into savings. In time we added other work options to our program.

We opened our first health center in 1973. That summer six black high school girls worked in the health center through the Leadership Development Program. That summer these girls got a glimpse of what they could make of their lives. Today Sarah Quinn is a registered nurse; Shirleen Phillips is a medical technologist; Mary Hardy has become a physical therapist; Andrea Phillips is in medical school. Because we took a constructive interest in developing these young women they have promising futures—careers that serve Jesus Christ and humanity.

One of the toughest aspects of leadership development is instilling a sense of responsibility. Young people who have always worked for other people and have sensed that they were somehow being exploited often develop a tendency to just "get by" in their work.

One day I was working with Larry Harper, one of the young men in the program. We were putting the finishing touches on a building. We had one part almost finished when Larry said, "This will do."

I answered, "Larry, we're not finished yet."

"But this is good enough," Larry insisted.

"Larry," I said, "we're doing this for ourselves. We own this building. It's ours. We want it to be the best we can make it. We want it to last. We don't want to have to come back and do this over right away."

I always insisted that the young people do their work well. Many had never been disciplined except out of anger. So when they came to work in a Christian environment they didn't expect to be corrected. When I corrected them, then, they felt that I was angry.

I had to just talk it into their heads that I wasn't angry, that I was just trying to help them learn to do their jobs well. Because these young people had long since lost their sense of self-worth and were just beginning to recover it through our love for them, we found it hard to provide the kind of discipline they needed. For many I became the father figure they never had, and that often meant being an authority they could rebel against as part of growing up.

One barrier to developing responsibility was that the young people lacked a sense of ownership. This was the major purpose of our savings plan. The young people in the program were required to put half their earnings into savings. These savings not only provided for future schooling but also provided the capital for the buildings they were constructing. When that sunk in, a sense of ownership of their work began to develop. Particularly among the poor who have owned so little, establishing ownership is a key to moving beyond a survival mentality to long-range planning.

I learned that to develop young leaders I had to help each person identify his gifts and skills, then find ways to sharpen them. As they developed their skills, their self-confidences grew.

Herbert had many skills. He was an excellent truck driver. Because he learned new skills so quickly, he became a great general handyman. For several years he directed a volunteer construction crew in a ministry of remodeling houses throughout the community. Then in 1971 he traveled all over the country to study youth work on a Ford Foundation Fellowship. The two years after that he studied at the Maryland Bible Institute.

While Herbert was gone I realized that my time to move on had come. Artis and Carolyn Fletcher, Dolphus and Rosie Weary, and Jimmy Walker were all back in Mendenhall directing the programs. In 12 years I had fulfilled my goal of leadership development in Mendenhall. I needed to move out of the way to give these young leaders room to grow. The Mendenhall church commissioned H. P. Spees and me and our families to start a ministry in Jackson, and we were off.

In 1974 Herbert joined us in Jackson. He headed up People's Development, Inc., a housing construction ministry. Before long he opened a youth center which we named after him. Herbert had become a strong and effective leader—a key member of our staff.

Leadership development continued to have a central place in our ministry at Jackson. We had several students attending Jackson State University who participated in our Leadership Development Program. We helped each student develop his or her ministry. Some have now moved into these ministries full time. Joan works in the journalism department. Eva is a bookkeeper. Derek, along with Don Strohnbehn, runs Harambee House where they live with and disciple four boys from bad home situations.

As our Jackson ministry developed we began to ask ourselves how we could help the rest of the nation with leadership development. Young volunteers were coming to work among us and to learn from us for weeks or months at a time. How could we train these young people so they could provide leadership in their home communities? In response to this need, in 1978 we opened the John M. Perkins International Study Center to train future leaders from across the country and from third-world nations in strategies of Christian community development.

The program, directed by Tim Robertson, combines classroom instruction, field work, and independent study. Classroom instruction focuses on three areas: community development, the black experience, and the history and vision of Voice of Calvary.

Each student gains practical experience through working in a development project such as church planting, personal evangelism, health care, housing development, youth work, development of economic enterprises, or adult education. Students are matched with projects on the basis of each student's interests and abilities and the needs of his home community.

In August of 1979, Herbert Jones went to be with the Lord. Herbert's life symbolized the lasting fruit of leadership development. Today a new crop of leaders who grew up under Herbert's loving care are moving into ministries of their own. The things I heard from my teachers I passed along to faithful men like Herbert, who in turn taught others.

In the spring of 1981 it became clear that I had once again worked myself out of a job. A new team of leaders in Jackson was providing strong, effective leadership to the ministry. It was time for me to move on. Lem Tucker replaced me as president of Voice of Calvary Ministries.

In my 20 years of developing community leaders I had discovered some simple, but crucial principles.

Leadership development is the key to the continuation and growth of a ministry. Jesus said, "You did not choose me, but I chose you to go and bear fruit—fruit that will last" (John 15:16, *NIV*). I am convinced that the key to bearing lasting fruit is not in developing programs but in developing people— leaders. I believe that developing creative leaders is both the most essential and the most difficult part of community development. It was the heart of Jesus' strategy. It must be the center of our strategy too.

Leadership develops in an environment of freedom and accountability. For a young person to learn to take responsibility, he must be given responsibility and the authority to fulfill it. At the same time he needs to be accountable to someone in authority to do the job and do it well. Strong leadership will seldom develop without this kind of accountability to authority.

Well-designed programs can increase a leader's effectiveness. Experience has taught us that a well-designed program is built around people in two ways. First, the program is created as a response to the needs of the people; it is not just someone's idea of something that might be nice to do. Second, a well-designed program is structured so that the people in the community can lead it themselves. A program shaped around both the *needs* and the *leadership skills* in the community can be a valuable tool in the hands of the right people.

Communities need a broad base of leadership. When I speak on the lack of black leadership, people respond, "What about Jesse Jackson? What about Reverend Sullivan?"

Yes, in every city we have a few outstanding leaders; but what we need is to raise up a broad base of leadership in business, in education, in health care, and a host of other areas in every community. The media tends to try to define black leadership as the highly visible few. This hinders the development of a broad base of leadership. The black community must not accept that narrow definition of leadership.

Another barrier to developing this broad base of leaders is that debate within the black community on which strategies to adopt is discouraged. The present leaders seem to fear that others will interpret this debate as disunity, and that the black voice will be weakened. So young leaders often find only one option for how to serve—to fall in line with the existing leadership structure. This lack of freedom to debate discourages the development of creative, new approaches to solving our problems. We must move beyond these limitations to raise up from among our own ranks a whole army of new young leaders in this generation. Without doing this there is no hope of making a lasting difference in our neediest communities.

We need leaders. Leaders with a faith that sees the depth of our needs, yet persists in believing in the power of the gospel. Leaders with a hope which can see the future and move others toward it. Leaders with a love that will sacrifice self in order to serve others.

If we are to have that kind of leader we dare not leave leadership development to chance. We must make the discipling of new leaders the very center of our ministry strategy.

REFLECTION

1. The author's strategy of leadership development grew out of the needs of the community where he ministered. Compare or contrast the availability of leadership in your com-

munity to that which existed in Mendenhall in the early sixties.

If there are significant differences between the two communities, how might those translate into differences in a leadership development program? Should it take more or less time to turn out strong Christian leaders in your community than it did in Mendenhall? Why?

2. Scan the chapter, singling out four or more principles of leadership development that would apply in any community. How many of these principles have you seen at work in your own life?

3. Assume that you are matched with a Christian teen and assigned the task of developing him into a strong Christian leader over the next five years. What would your strategy be?

4. What priority do you think leadership development should be in a strategy of Christian community development? Is it a must? An option? Why?

8
GETTING YOUR FEET WET

It was as though I had read his thoughts.

The year was 1972. H. P. Spees and I were sitting in front of our little church building in Mendenhall. "H.," as his friends called him, and five other young people had come from Glendale Presbyterian Church in California to work with us for eight weeks that summer. Six of those eight weeks were behind us.

H.'s thoughts were filled with what he had seen and felt during those six weeks. Our biggest project had been building our gym and educational building, so H. and the others had been working on that. They had done a little tutoring too. But mostly what was on H.'s mind was the people—people who had so little, people who needed so much, people without the gospel. And in getting a close firsthand look at Voice of Calvary Ministries, H. had also caught a vision of hope. Here was a ministry which offered the answer to these needs. Here was a practical, workable way to give the gospel hands and feet to reach out to those who needed it.

I turned to H. "How would you like to come back and work with me?"

H.'s eyes lit up and a half-smile surfaced. "John, ever since I got here that's just what I've been dreaming of."

H.'s commitment to give his life to serving Christ by bringing the gospel to the poor didn't come out of a vacuum. It took place in a setting especially designed for that kind of response—Voice of Calvary's volunteer program.

From the very first, volunteers have filled an important place in VOC's ministry. The first volunteers who came were blacks like Momma Wilson and Sister Carroway from California who worked with us to reach out into the community. Then when we organized our Bible Institute, some white ministers came to share in the teaching, though they had to withdraw later due to white pressure.

A few whites such as Reverend John MacArthur, Jr., from Burbank, California, came to help with evangelistic programs in the schools. I think the kinship John and I developed was one reason for such a great response. For a black man and a white man to share Christ together in Mississippi was a mighty witness to the gospel's power. John was here when Dr. Martin Luther King was killed. Schools where we had already spoken together called and asked us to come back. With so much hostility in the air, they knew the students needed to see this living example of the gospel's reconciling power.

More volunteers came in the late sixties. With school integration finally coming to Mississippi, these summer volunteers held what we called "freedom schools." These were to prepare black students to compete in what was for them an entirely new environment and culture.

Then came the great confrontations in Mendenhall and Brandon when some of us were beaten by the Mississippi highway patrol. The summer after that, in 1971, we had our first major groups of black and white volunteers together. The blacks came from the cities, bringing a commitment to social and economic justice and a determination to make a difference for their people. But they also brought a certain amount of anger growing out of their own oppression and the events of the sixties.

The white volunteers came from the suburbs. Though eager to share Christ they lacked social awareness. We had hoped that the summer program would bring together evangelical whites and socially committed blacks. But in an atmosphere heavily overcast with Dr. King's death and electrified with racial confrontations in Mendenhall and Brandon, it didn't work. It was disastrous. Despite this false start we remained convinced of the need to bring blacks and whites together to work in communities of need, modeling a gospel of reconciliation. Confident God would make it work, we tried again.

The next summer a group of young people came from California. That group included H. Spees and Terry—now his wife. During that summer H.'s vision for his own life was transformed. The next year H. joined our staff. They have been with us ever since. Their present ministry is breaking through racial barriers in my own hometown of New Hebron, Mississippi; whites and blacks work together to meet needs they all share. Their work demonstrates what the gospel of Jesus Christ can do in people's lives.

Our volunteer program today offers Christians an opportunity both to serve and to learn. A volunteer brings to our ministry for a time his gifts and skills and employs them to empower the people. Our ministry depends heavily on volunteers who tutor, cook for our nutrition program, do construction work, conduct vacation Bible schools, and work in our health centers, our thrift stores and print shop. Without them, much that VOC has accomplished would never have been possible.

In 1975 I challenged the students at Wheaton College with the need for a preschool in Mendenhall. I looked up a few months later at Steve Hayes, a young black man, and Debbie Hale, a young white woman, who had come down to spend a year surveying the needs of the community. They stayed on the next year and launched our Genesis One project. At the end of that year they left, turning a thriving preschool over to indigenous black leadership.

Over the years volunteers have given our ministry credibility in the minds of the local people. Community residents see that people who love Christ have come hundreds or thousands of miles to sacrifice their time and energy. They see the diligence and faithfulness of the volunteers. Then they may discover that the volunteers aren't being paid to do this. That life testimony says a lot to the community about Christ's love and the integrity of the ministry.

As much as we need and appreciate the work the volunteers do, most volunteers go home feeling they have received more than they have given. For many, their weeks, months, or years at Voice of Calvary have been a learning experience second to none.

They learn, first of all, *to know the needs of the people in human terms.* The impersonal poverty statistics take on names and faces. They become friends, people with feelings— feelings the volunteer can, at least to some degree, share.

Second, by serving as part of an effective, ongoing ministry, the volunteers *catch a vision for the power of the gospel to meet these needs.* They begin to understand the holistic nature of the gospel. They start to pick up the basics of our ministry strategy. They see a wide variety of methods through which the gospel can be brought alive to people. To make the volunteers' stay as profitable as possible, we supplement their fieldwork with seminars and individual study which help them understand our mission and strategy.

A third thing volunteers learn is *the meaning of reconciliation.* Most volunteers have never before worked in a church or ministry where blacks and whites work hand in hand as a dynamic spiritual team. Many bring with them feelings of guilt or blame which they need to work through. They leave with a new awareness of the need for reconciliation within the church, a new confidence that the church can be reconciled, and an elementary understanding of how to move toward that goal.

For some volunteers their time here serves yet a fourth learning purpose—*discerning something of God's call on their own lives.* Certainly seeing the need and catching a vision are part of this process; but for these volunteers it goes beyond that. As they work among us they find their hearts drawn to people with certain needs. They sense a growing conviction that God wants them to give their lives to serving them. They see how God uses their own gifts and skills in such a ministry. Their vision becomes personalized: this is what God can do through *me.*

Some volunteers come to clarify a present call and to prepare themselves to fulfill it. Others have concern for the poor and just want to test the waters—get their feet wet—to see if they belong in this kind of work. To still others, who have never considered long-term ministry among the poor, God's call comes as a surprise.

The most significant fruit of our volunteer program is that volunteers have gone on to find a deeper meaning in life through service to God and others. Besides H. and Terry, a number of other volunteers have joined VOC staff. Eva Meyers is taking over Vera Mae's place as the director of our Child Evangelism Fellowship program. Paul Lundquist is now the financial director for our health services. Donna Wheeler came as a volunteer three years ago and stayed on to eventually become my personal secretary. Fred Shaw is the assistant manager of our cooperative farm in Mendenhall.

Former volunteers whose time with us changed the direction of their lives now dot our nation. After graduating from Wheaton, Ben Johnson, Jr., worked in our medical lab for two years as a technician. While here he decided to go to medical school. He now is a medical doctor in Chicago. Dana Shaw directs a ministry in the inner city of Pittsburgh. Mary Bucher is now a nurse in Macon, Mississippi. And the list could go on and on.

Even for someone who has no sense of call to relocate among the poor, volunteering is an experience not to be missed. Not only can the volunteer offer his gifts and skills for a time, but he can bring his new understanding and vision back to his home church and help them to shape a meaningful Christian response to the cries of the needy. I consistently find that those churches which respond most compassionately to the needy are those which have sent out from their own congregations people to live and walk and eat and breathe among the poor, and who have then heard their eyewitness accounts of the need, the opportunity, and the challenge. Not only do ministries like VOC need volunteers; our churches need the firsthand involvement with the needy that volunteering provides.

The volunteering experience can take several forms. At VOC we host volunteer groups, short-term volunteers, a summer volunteer program, and a one-year study center program.

Church or college groups of up to 15 people can come to work for one or two weeks. These groups provide volunteer labor in housing renovation, mailings, secretarial work, child evangelism, vacation Bible schools, and other projects. They learn about and participate in holistic community development on a very practical level.

Short-term volunteers come to share their skills and energy for less than a year. They work in such areas as housing renovation, Thriftco, office work, communications, child evangelism, health center, youth center, tutoring, construction and maintenance, and printing. Some older and retired people share their experiences and skills in this way.

The summer volunteer program is for college students and career people. Through this program, about 25 young people each summer work in direct contact with the community through such projects as child evangelism, youth recreation, tutoring, housing renovation, and other similar activities. Seminars and Bible studies to stimulate spiritual growth are integral to the program.

The John M. Perkins International Study Center offers opportunities to learn in both theory and practice what Voice of Calvary has discovered about Christian community development. This one-year program equips its students to return to communities of need to implement a holistic strategy of Christian community development. Students learn through on-the-job experience as well as seminar sessions and field trips.

Voice of Calvary looks for three qualities in prospective volunteers: (1) *The lordship of Christ*—a life centered in prayer and in God's Word is the most important requirement of any volunteer; (2) *Servanthood*—Mark 9:35 tells us: "If anyone wants to be first, he shall be last of all, and servant of all." While good stewardship demands that we use our gifts and talents, no job is too menial for anyone. (3) *Fellowship*—volunteers should have a real desire to share in the life of our local fellowship. This responsibility includes a concern for the needs of others in the Body and a sense of accountability to the church leadership.

For more information on volunteering at VOC, or for a volunteer application, write:

Coordinator of Volunteer Services
Voice of Calvary Ministries
Box 10562
1655 St. Charles Street
Jackson, MS 39209

Many ministries throughout the country welcome volunteers. There may be one in your area that would prove to be both a good mission opportunity and training resource for people in your own church. Several denominations, such as the Church of the Brethren, the Mennonites, and the Friends have extensive volunteer programs which are open to people of other denominations.

I would like to challenge every denomination to create at the national or international level an agency to provide opportunities for young people to work in ministries which are communicating a holistic gospel to the people they serve. Beyond that, I dream of an effective interdenominational, evangelical Christian peace corps for America through which young people, black and white, would commit three years of their lives to taking the good news of salvation through Jesus Christ to the neediest in our land.

I do not believe that volunteering should be primarily the response of an individual; at its best, volunteering is the response of a church. Before a volunteer comes to VOC, we send a letter to the volunteer's pastor requesting that the church commission the volunteer as a short-term missionary of that congregation. I like to see the whole church share in sending the volunteer. While some volunteers are reluctant to ask their church to help with their expenses, I believe it is important *to the home church* to support the volunteer both with finances and prayers, much as the church would support any other missionary it sends out. The volunteer needs to know that he is not just a "lone ranger," but that he is being sent as a missionary of his local church.

When the volunteer returns home, then, he is responsible to report back to his church the account of his experience just as Paul and Barnabas reported back to their home church in Antioch after their missionary journey. In this way the whole church shares in the missionary's joys and pains. The volunteer becomes the eyes and ears of the church among the poor, transmitting to them the needs he has seen and his vision for how the church can respond.

As with any good thing, volunteering is not without its potential problems.

One danger is that a volunteer will come more to meet his own need than to minister to the needs of others. Affluent Christians may be drawn to work with the poor because they feel guilty about their own abundance. White Christians may be motivated to work among blacks to try to atone for racial injustices. Such volunteers may find themselves so preoccupied with trying to relieve their own guilt that they fail to freely and wholeheartedly express Christ's love to those they are there to serve. While there is a legitimate "need to serve," we must be sure that the needs of those we are serving, not our own needs, set the agenda. Otherwise we are not servants, but exploiters.

Another problem is that some volunteers, upon coming to a fellowship like VOC where decisions are normally made by consensus, expect to immediately have an equal voice in planning and policy decisions. Many white volunteers, in particular, seem to question the decisions of black leaders more than they do the decisions of white leaders. They require black leaders to prove their competence before they will trust their leadership. Submitting to black leadership is one of the toughest things for many volunteers to learn to do.

A white store owner betrayed his disbelief a while back when I directed one of our white volunteers to carry my purchases out of the store. "We're just reversing roles," I replied in mock seriousness. "He's my slave."

The storeowner's astonishment typifies a deep-seated and subtle prejudice present in many white Americans. This prejudice is grounded in the often unconscious assumption that the historical dominance of whites over blacks in America has some inherent validity. White volunteers are often surprised to find this attitude surfacing in themselves when they come under a black leader's authority. But for the races to be reconciled, whites will have to confront and overcome this expectation of being in authority. Especially in black community development, whites need to be able to submit to and strongly support the leadership of black leaders. Whites wanting to minister in black communities need to consider actually seeking out indigenous blacks whose lead they can follow. Volunteering can give whites their first experience of submitting to black leadership and help to identify any latent prejudice that needs to be dealt with.

Volunteering, even though it is not problem free, provides one of the best possible ways for your church to help take the gospel to one of our greatest mission fields—the poor of America. They need the gifts and skills you can bring; you and your church need the compassion and the vision that volunteering can inspire.

I extend to you this special invitation: join us in Mississippi as we reach out into this racially torn world, demonstrating the unifying power of the gospel. Or go to your own inner city or to the rural poor of your state and stand alongside those who are proclaiming the gospel there.

I call young black Christians and believers of other ethnic groups to bring your empathy to the needs of oppressed people. I call white middle-class churches and colleges to send your young people to places where they can touch the lives of others.

I invite you to let Jesus reach out through you to touch the lives of the poor.

REFLECTION

1. For what kinds of reasons do people volunteer to spend a few days, weeks, or months ministering to the poor?
2. How does volunteering benefit the poor? The volunteer? The volunteer's home church?
3. What are some potential problems with volunteering?
4. What ministries to the poor already exist in your state? In neighboring states? What ministries to the poor does your own denomination have in the U.S.? Of these ministries, select the two or three where you would be most interested in volunteering, either individually or as part of a church volunteer group. Write them for additional information on their ministries and inquire about the possibility of volunteering. Ask God's direction in whether you should volunteer with one of these ministries in the near future.

9

RELOCATION: A STRATEGY FOR HERE AND NOW

Our response to the poor is a crucial test of our faithfulness to the gospel.

"The Spirit of the Lord is upon Me," Jesus read, "because He anointed Me to preach the gospel to the poor. He has sent Me to proclaim release to the captives, and recovery of sight to the blind, to set free those who are downtrodden, to proclaim the favorable year of the Lord" (Luke 4:18,19).

The church, as Christ's Body on earth, is charged with carrying out Christ's mission. Jesus' example is our model, our biblical mandate to proclaim the Good News to the poor.

When at the judgment Jesus rewards those who have faithfully lived out the gospel, they will respond, "Lord, when did we see You hungry, and feed You, or thirsty, and give You drink? And when did we see You a stranger, and invite You in, or naked, and clothe You?" Jesus will reply, "Truly I say to you, to the extent that you did it to one of these brothers of Mine, even the least of them, you did it to Me" (Matt. 25:37,38,40). Their compassion for the poor and oppressed will have been a natural outworking of their faith.

On the other hand, those who do not live out the gospel will be damned. This brazen bunch of self-righteous religious people will ask, "Lord, when did we see You hungry . . . and did not take care of You?" (Matt. 25:44).

To be the church is to be the first group.

John the Baptist sent his disciples to ask Jesus, "Are You the [expected] One, or shall we look for someone else?" Jesus in effect answered, "My actions speak for themselves." "Go and report to John the things which you hear and see: the blind receive sight and the lame walk, the lepers are cleansed and the deaf hear, and the dead are raised up, and the poor have the gospel preached to them" (Matt. 11:3-5). His works testified that Jesus was indeed the Messiah. The same test applies to us today. If someone were to come to your church and ask, "Is the Christ here or do we need to look somewhere else?" what answer would your actions give?

When I speak at colleges and universities about ministering to the poor, students often ask, "What about the rich?"

Jesus certainly put no restrictions on the Great Commission. We must take the gospel to everyone. Yet Jesus, by both word and action, showed that the poor have a special place in God's plan. Both testaments consistently sound the theme of God's special concern for the poor.

"All my bones will exclaim, 'Yahweh, who can compare with you in rescuing the poor man from the stronger, the needy from the man who exploits him?' " (Psa. 35:10, *JB*).

"The righteous is concerned for the rights of the poor, the wicked does not understand such concern" (Prov. 29:7).

"Open your mouth for the dumb, for the rights of all the unfortunate. Open your mouth, judge righteously, and defend the rights of the afflicted and needy" (Prov. 31:8,9).

"Then I looked again at all the acts of oppression which were being done under the sun. And behold I saw the tears of the oppressed and that they had no one to comfort them; and on the side of their oppressors was power, but they had no one to comfort them" (Eccl. 4:1).

"They only asked us to remember the poor—the very thing I also was eager to do" (Gal. 2:10).

"But whoever has the world's goods, and beholds his brother in need and closes his heart against him, how does the love of God abide in him" (1 John 3:17).

As God's agents on earth, we are responsible to live out this special concern for the poor. You cannot be and you ought not to be in the president's administration unless you are committed to the president's philosophy. Otherwise his program will not be carried out smoothly. In the same way you cannot effectively carry out God's program unless you have the mind of Christ. To have the mind of Christ is to be especially concerned with the poor. It is to have a special compassion for the disenfranchised, for the aching in our society. And it is to act on that concern.

Whether we take the gospel to the poor, then, is not an incidental side issue; it is a revealing test of the church's faithfulness to Christ's mission.

How then shall we proclaim Good News to the poor? Once again Jesus is our model. "The Word became flesh, and dwelt among us, and we beheld His glory, glory as of the only begotten from the Father, full of grace and truth" (John 1:14). Jesus relocated. He didn't commute to earth one day a week and shoot back up to heaven. He left His throne and became one of us so that we might see the life of God revealed in Him.

Paul says that we are to have this same attitude Jesus expressed when He humbled Himself: "Have this attitude in yourselves which was also in Christ Jesus, who, although He existed in the form of God, did not regard equality with God a thing to be grasped, but emptied Himself, taking the form of a bond-servant, and being made in the likeness of men. And being found in appearance as a man, He humbled Himself by becoming obedient to the point of death, even death on a cross" (Phil. 2:5-8).

Jesus was equal with God, yet He gave that up and took on the form of a servant. He took on the likeness of man. He came and lived among us. He was called Immanuel—"God with us." The incarnation is the ultimate relocation.

Not only is the incarnation relocation; relocation is also incarnation. That is, not only did God relocate among us by taking the form of a man, but when a fellowship of believers relocates into a community, Christ incarnate invades that community. Christ, as His Body, as His church, comes to dwell there.

Relocating among the poor flies in the face of the materialism of middle America. To consider relocating, then, forces us to confront our own values. Have we accepted the world's values of upward mobility? Or have we accepted God's values as demonstrated in the life of Jesus Christ? That's the issue.

As I speak around the country, some people find my words on relocation hard to accept. They ask, "Do all have to relocate?"

I answer, "Only those who are called have to relocate." Then I add, "But if you're asking the question too angrily, then you may be called. If you are uneasy about it, God may be calling you."

If you resist the suggestion to relocate, you need to ask, "Why don't I want to go and live among the poor and wretched of the earth?" Ask yourself that question several times. Your answer will be the reason you ought to go.

If you have children you may answer, "The kids in that neighborhood don't get a good education." Then that's why you need to go. You've just discovered a need! In moving to the neighborhood, their need would become your need. The families in that community need others to feel that need with them, to make it their very own, to do something to improve the quality of education.

You might start a tutoring program, a preschool, a summer enrichment program, or even an elementary school. Whatever method you choose will grow out of relocating.

Now I'm not asking you to sacrifice your children. God gave us our children. They need a good education. If they can't get one in the public schools, find another option. On the other hand, don't overlook the educational advantages of sending your child to the neighborhood school. Their increased understanding of the needs and culture of the neighborhood and the friendships they form may more than offset anything they give up academically.

Maybe you don't want to move into the neighborhood because of crime. Then that's why you need to go. You've just found another need. Go identify with the people, help them understand the reasons behind the crime. Then work with them to solve the problem. Once you've relocated, once you've become one of them, you're in a position to do that. People in an ethnic neighborhood may hate the police. Refuse to share their hate, however justified; instead, commit yourself to now and to the future.

Organize a neighborhood watch group. Sponsor crime prevention workshops. Build positive, cooperative relationships with the local police. Invite the chief of police or the policeman on your beat to talk with church or community groups. Through letters to the police department, affirm those who do a good job; hold accountable those who do a poor job. Involve the policeman on your beat in community affairs.

In the past, our St. Charles neighborhood in Jackson has had one of the highest, if not the highest, crime rates in Jackson. During the past year our community's presence and our crime prevention efforts have cut the crime rate in half in our neighborhood.

But you ask, "Can't a suburban Christian minister to those who are aching without becoming one with them?"

And I answer, "Why on earth do you suppose these people have a welfare mentality?" It's because outside "experts" have come up with programs that have retarded and dehumanized them. Yes, our best attempts to reach people from the outside will patronize them. Our best attempts will psychologically and socially damage them. We must live among them. We must become one with them. Their needs must become our needs.

The decision to relocate is a big decision, a decision to be made only in obedience to God's call. Relocation is not simple. It involves much more than moving to a different house. It requires careful preparation and a clear understanding of how to proceed after the move. And although each ministry will be uniquely shaped around both the gifts of the ministry team and the needs of the community, this basic strategy, with only slight variations, can guide the relocation process wherever it takes place.

Do volunteer work with an existing ministry to the poor. Find an existing ministry in your target neighborhood or a similar area where you can spend a few weeks as a volunteer. This is a great way to see the needs firsthand, to catch a vision for what can be done, to discover how God can best use your gifts to serve the poor. It gives God an excellent opportunity to clarify or confirm what He is calling you to do.

Share your vision with your church. As you prepare yourself for your ministry, you can be educating your church too. Ask your church to sponsor your group's ministry as a mission outreach if at all possible. Your church's involvement in your ministry can help them catch a greater vision for ministry to the poor.

Form your ministry team. A year or two before you make your actual move into the target neighborhood, form a team of several families whom God has called to the ministry, who all share a commitment to make the target neighborhood your home.

Build a sense of Christian community. Take this year or two of preparation to let the Holy Spirit shape you into a united team, a strong Christian community. Meet regularly as a group to pray, to plan, to dream, to bear one another's burdens.

Consider sending one or two couples from your ministry team to receive special training. The International Study Center in Jackson, Mississippi offers a three-month training program designed especially for people who are preparing to relocate among the poor, particularly among American blacks. Additional volunteer experience can also be valuable at this stage.

Move into the community. All the families in your group should move into the same neighborhood. You may even want to all live in the same house, or, if that's not practical, in two houses, as a way to strengthen your sense of community.

It only makes sense to locate in a community which isn't going to be wiped out by urban renewal in 10 years. Community development has as its goal the long-term improvement of community conditions and the lives of people in the community. Your target area also needs to include possible sites for developing small businesses.

Go there to stay! Opposition will come. Expect it. Disappointments will come. Count on them. Whatever problems arise, work through them. Don't run from them. For example, when couples who have relocated in a poor community begin to have children, their parents often pressure them to move out of the neighborhood. Many families give up their commitment to the target community at this point. Expect this testing of your commitment. Be committed to staying. God will use your suffering to "perfect, confirm, strengthen and establish you" (1 Pet. 5:10).

Outline a community development target area. Decide on a geographical area where you will work to reclaim a sense of community. In a community of single-family homes on good-sized lots, your target area might be everything within a six-block radius. In a high-density population area with a lot of apartment buildings your target area would have to be much smaller.

Get a job, preferably within the community. You might create a job within the community if you have the skills. Live in the community, even if you must work outside of it.

Start a Bible study. When you first go into a community, start a Bible study. Best of all is to start it in one of the people's homes. If you can't do that, start it in your own home.

Listen to the people. After you've relocated and before you start any programs, listen. A little Chinese poem says:

> Go to the people
> Live among them
> Learn from them
> Love them
> Start with what they know
> Build on what they have:
> But of the best leaders
> When their task is accomplished
> Their work is done
> The people will remark,
> "We have done it ourselves."

Spend your first year listening and learning. Invite people over to your house, and don't take no for an answer. If they don't come, go to their houses. Visit people when they are sick.

Work with the neighborhood children. People love folks who love their children. Take young people along when you go places. Show them another part of town through your eyes.

From the beginning make it your goal to raise up indigenous leadership from the neighborhood who can take over your job from you in 10 years. Your job is not over until you've done that.

Teach them to love their community. Find good things to say about it. Talk about the trees. If there is a lot of crime, talk about how good it could be if it weren't for this crime. Always be positive. Of course the very fact that you have chosen to move there is a powerful positive statement to them.

You'll never get young people to come back to provide leadership for their community by being negative. They will come back only because they feel good about the people, because they love the community they're coming back to. They have to come to love their own ghetto.

Join or establish a church in the immediate area. Do this before you begin any programs. Your whole ministry should be rooted in the church. The church will not operate every program or own every service, but the church will be the catalyst to get them started.

If there is a church in the area which preaches the gospel, whose pastor lives in the community and has a vision for its renewal, you might consider making it your base of ministry. Or you can start your own church in your home. As it grows you can move to a big basement or a rented building. Plan from the beginning not to put a lot of money into a meeting place. Put your money into developing the community.

Respond to the needs. Only after you have lived among the people, identified their most deeply felt needs, and established a church base are you ready to develop programs. Don't provide services *for* the people; develop community-based responses to their needs *with* them. Provide leadership, but let the programs belong to the people.

There it is—a strategy of relocation for here and now. Is God calling you to go? I want to challenge suburban whites and successful, well-educated blacks, American Indians and Orientals—Christians of every race—to consider your response to the poor. God's charge is clear:

"The kind of fasting I want is this: Remove the chains of oppression and the yoke of injustice, and let the oppressed go free. Share your food with the hungry and open your homes to the homeless poor. Give clothes to those who have nothing to wear, and do not refuse to help your own relatives.

"Then my favor will shine on you like the morning sun, and your wounds will be quickly healed. I will always be with you to save you; my presence will protect you on every side. When you pray, I will answer you. When you call to me, I will respond.

"If you put an end to oppression, to every gesture of contempt, and to every evil word; if you give food to the hungry and satisfy those who are in need, then the darkness around you will turn to the brightness of noon. And I will always guide you and satisfy you with good things. I will keep you strong and well. You will be like a garden that has plenty of water, like a spring of water that never goes dry. Your people will rebuild what has long been in ruins, building again on the old foundations. You will be known as the people who rebuilt the walls, who restored the ruined houses" (Isaiah 58:6-12, *TEV*).

My dream is to see ministry teams all over our nation relocating into our ghettos, our Indian reservations, our depressed rural areas. My dream is to see these teams be Christ in those communities, proclaiming a holistic gospel by word and action, and by God's power bringing healing and wholeness to those among us who hurt the most.

My dream is for the church to proclaim the Good News to the poor.

REFLECTION

1. This chapter begins, "Our response to the poor is a crucial test of our faithfulness to the gospel." Do you believe that Scripture supports this statement? Why or why not?
2. What does the author mean when he says, "Not only is the incarnation relocation; relocation is also incarnation"?
3. How does relocating among the poor fly in the face of the materialism of middle America?

4. Assume that your church has decided to launch a ministry to the poor in your city or a nearby community. The church has pledged to help three or four church families relocate in the community of need as their missionary representatives. What first practical steps would your church and the ministry team need to take to establish such a ministry?
5. What neighborhoods or rural communities near you might be good locations for this kind of ministry?
6. Are you willing to be a part of such a ministry as either a member of the missionary team which relocates, or by actively supporting such a missionary team as part of the sending church?

THE STRATEGY

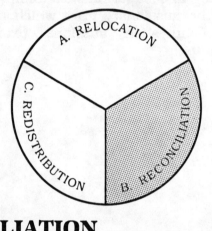

RECONCILIATION

10

LOVE IS STRONGER THAN HATE

That was the night God gave me a real compassion for whites—the night those Mississippi police officers beat me almost to death.

It was Saturday, February 7, 1970, about 6:30 p.m. The sun was just going down. Two vans driven by Louise Fox and Doug Huemmer were returning students to Tougaloo College near Jackson from Mendenhall where they had joined us in a civil rights march. In Plain, Mississippi, a few miles after the vans rolled over the line separating Simpson County from Rankins County, the highway patrol car that had trailed them from Mendenhall flashed on its blue lights and cut in between the two vans signaling for Doug to pull over.

A few minutes later our phone was ringing. It was Louise. "The people in Doug's van have been taken to the Brandon jail."

Reverend Curry Brown, Joe Paul Buckley and I set out for the Rankin County Jail in Brandon to set bail for Doug and his group.

During the 45-minute drive up highway 49 my mind churned. Why had the policeman let Louise go? To call me?

Was it a trap? Was another ambush waiting for us on highway 49?

We got to the county courthouse and jail and a highway patrolman showed us where to park. We had met no ambush on the highway. We got out of the car and told the patrolman, "We'd like to see the sheriff."

"Okay," he said. "You stay here and I'll go tell him you're here." Moments later out of the building came not Sheriff Edwards but a dozen highway patrolmen. They searched us, arrested us and even before they got us to the building started beating us. It was an ambush after all!

Inside the jail house the nightmare only got worse. At least five deputy sheriffs and seven to twelve highway patrolmen went to work on us. Sheriff Edwards joined in.

Here's how I described that scene later in the court trial: "When I got to the jail and saw the people in jail, of course I was horrified as to why we were arrested and when I got in the jail Sheriff Jonathan Edwards came over to me right away and said, 'This is the smart nigger, and this is a new ballgame. You're not in Simpson County now; you are in Brandon.' . . . He began to beat me, and from that time on they continued beating me. I was just beat to the floor and just punched and really beaten."[8]

Manorris Odom, one of the Tougaloo students there, testified that Sheriff Edwards beat me so hard that his "shirt tail came out."[9] During the beatings I tried to cover my head with my arms, but they beat me anyway till I was lying on the floor. Even then they just kept on beating and stomping me, kicking me in the head, in the ribs, in the groin. I rolled up into a ball to protect myself as best I could. And the beatings just went on and on.

It got worse as the night wore on. One officer brought a fork over to me and said, "Do you see this?" And he jammed it up my nose. Then he crammed it down my throat. Then they beat me to the ground again and stomped on me.

Because I was unconscious a lot of the time I don't remember a whole lot about the others. I do know that Doug and some of the students were beaten, and that Curry probably suffered the most of any of us.

And I remember their faces—so twisted with hate. It was

like looking at white-faced demons. For the first time I saw
what hate had done to those people. These policemen were
poor. They saw themselves as failures. The only way they
knew how to find a sense of worth was by beating us. Their
racism made them feel like "somebody."

When I saw that, I just couldn't hate back. I could only pity
them. I said to God that night, "God, if you will let me get out
of this jail alive"—and I really didn't think I would, maybe I
was trying to bargain with Him—"I really want to preach a
gospel that will heal these people, too."

Well, although the students who watched over me through
the night in that jail cell were sure for a while that I was dead
or about to die, I came out alive—and with a new call. My call
to preach the gospel now extended to whites.

That night in the Brandon jail I had for the first time seen
how the white man was a victim of his own racism. For the
first time I wanted to bring him a gospel that could set him
free. But that was only a start. I still harbored in my heart a
deep-seated bitterness against whites for all they had done to
me and my family. It went back to that night when Clyde was
shot. Back beyond that to my mother's death. As my case went
through the Mississippi courts and the majority of judges
proved to be just as racist as the policemen who had almost
killed me, my bitterness grew. There was no justice for a black
man!

My beating and the frustration and bitterness that followed took their toll. In July of 1970 I had a heart attack. I was
hospitalized in Mound Bayou, a small black community where
I had helped organize some co-ops. After a partial recovery I
found myself back in the same hospital with ulcers. Dr. Har-
vey Sanders, a black doctor, had to take out two-thirds of my
stomach.

Lying in that hospital bed I had a lot of time to think. I
thought about blacks and whites. About how, in a country
that claimed to stand for "liberty and justice for all," a black
man in Mississippi could get no justice. I thought about how
in Mississippi, "Christians" were the most racist whites of all.
How white preachers were in on most of the murders of civil
rights leaders. How Sunday School teachers were leading
members of the Klan. I thought of how the white "Christian"

businessmen supported the whole economic system which exploited blacks. And I began to think that maybe there was only one way to go—to give up on whites and white Christians and just work for me and mine.

I could start a little gospel radio station right there in Mound Bayou that would broadcast to the blacks all through the delta area. I could feature Bible preaching and good gospel music, and Vera Mae and I could live here in Mound Bayou where there were no more than half a dozen whites. We could just leave all that struggle behind us.

But when I was most tempted to give up, about to decide that the gospel couldn't reconcile—at least not in Mendenhall, two doctors administered healing to my spirit even as they cared for my body. Dr. Joanne Roberts, one of the few white persons in the center, and Dr. Sanders, a black, were themselves images of hope—living examples of reconciliation.

Hope began to flicker again.

I thought of the white people in Mendenhall who had not bowed their knees to Baal. There was Mr. Neely, the head of the savings and loan who had gotten blacks to save there, and blacks had benefited from it. When many people involved in the civil rights movement had trouble getting credit, Mr. Neely never turned his back on us.

There was Mr. Boyles who carried our insurance. While other churches lost their insurance because they were involved in civil rights, we didn't lose insurance on anything—our church building, our car, or any of our facilities—because Mr. Boyles stuck with us.

And then there was Mr. Barnett, a blacksmith and piano tuner. Growing up in the black community of Hawlpond, he had sung gospel music in black churches. Probably because of the friendships he formed growing up, he never turned his back on blacks. He helped us put our old school bus body on a new chassis, tuned up our piano, and supported us every way he could.

So a few white people in Mendenhall stood out as glimmers of hope. And even when things looked darkest, when I most wanted to run, I couldn't get away from my new call—God had called me to take the gospel to whites, too.

The Spirit of God worked on me as I lay in that bed. An

image formed in my mind—the image of a cross, of Christ on the cross. This Jesus knew what I had suffered. He understood. He cared. Because He had gone through it all Himself.

He too was arrested and falsely accused. He too had an unjust trial. He too was beaten. Then He was nailed to a cross and killed like a common criminal. But when He looked at the mob who had crucified Him, He didn't hate them; He loved them! And He prayed, "Father forgive them; for they do not know what they are doing" (Luke 23:34).

His enemies hated, but He forgave. God wouldn't let me escape that. He showed me that however unjustly I had been treated, in my bitterness and hatred I was just as sinful as those who had beaten me. And I needed forgiveness for my bitterness.

I read Matthew 6:14,15 again and again in that bed: "For if you forgive men for their transgressions, your heavenly Father will also forgive you. But if you do not forgive men, then your Father will not forgive your transgressions." To receive God's forgiveness, I was going to have to forgive those who had hurt me. As I prayed, the faces of those policemen passed before me one by one, and I forgave each one. Faces of other white people from the past came before me, and I forgave them. I could sense that God was working a deep inner healing in me that went far back beyond February 7, 1970. It went clear back to my earliest memories of childhood. God was healing all those wounds that had kept me from loving whites. How sweet God's forgiveness and healing was!

As soon as that happened I saw how these unhealed memories had limited God's will. I recalled a scene from 12 or 13 years before. I was still in California. God had just started talking to me about coming back to Mississippi. It was on one of those days that I went with the Christian businessmen to share my testimony in a prison camp. As the car climbed that Southern California mountain road I turned to Ed Anthony beside me. "Ed, God is calling me to preach the gospel to black people."

"John," he responded, "God may be calling you to preach the gospel to everybody—not just blacks." When Ed said that, I don't think I fully understood how much he was saying.

I came to Mississippi convinced that because of the historical oppression of my people, God was calling me to preach the gospel especially to blacks. My whole drive for those first 10 years was to lift blacks from their oppression. I heard the voices calling for black self-determination and black liberation, and accepted that. What I really wanted in the sixties was for the white man to leave us alone, to let us be. Because of the hostility, I had very little contact with the white Mississippi community.

Even as I felt this way, I knew in my mind that the gospel was supposed to reconcile people across economic, racial, and social barriers. But that all just seemed theoretical until Brandon. At Brandon God showed me how racism had psychologically damaged whites just as much as it had blacks. Through those sick men, God showed me the need to take a gospel of love to whites filled with hate.

I was beginning to understand what Ed Anthony meant. The same gospel that frees blacks also frees whites. You can't free one without the other. I was beginning to see what Martin Luther King saw long before: our destiny was tied to their destiny. What liberated me liberated them; what liberated them liberated me.

Demanding our rights had not softened the white community as we hoped it would. Instead, it had stiffened their opposition. Lying there on my bed I was able to see that confronting white people with hostility was only going to create war. If there was going to be any healing it would have to take place in an atmosphere of love. I had been trying to demand justice. Now God was opening my eyes to a new and better strategy— seeking reconciliation. I could not bring justice for other people. As a Christian, my responsibility was to seek to be reconciled. Then out of that reconciliation, justice would flow.

Affirmative action, integration, and so on, might be useful, but they alone were not justice. Real justice would never be achieved by passing laws or going to court. "Many seek the ruler's favor, but justice for man comes from the Lord" (Prov. 29:26). True justice could come only as people's hearts were made right with God and God's love motivated them to be reconciled to each other.

Now that God had enabled me to forgive the many whites who had wronged me, I found myself able to truly love them. I wanted to return good for evil. In my own life God had cleansed away bitterness and hatred and replaced it with love. If He could do that in my life, He could do it in other people too—whether black or white.

A hope began to take root. God could heal the bitterness of blacks and replace it with forgiveness. God could forgive whites. He could move them beyond guilt-motivated patronization to responsible partnership with blacks in working for justice. How that could be achieved I didn't know. But God called me. He gave me the dream. He would make it happen.

Well, the doctor said that I needed to put some distance between myself and the stress in Mendenhall. So when I got out of the hospital Vera Mae and I moved to Jackson. Dolphus took over as executive director at Mendenhall. I worked on several projects in Jackson—consulting work with poverty programs, business development projects, and so forth. So I had plenty to do. And we kept going back to VOC in Mendenhall for church.

Then for a year in '72 and '73, I traveled across the country on a Ford Foundation Fellowship studying community development. I observed Reverend Leon Sullivan's work with Opportunities Industrial Corporation in Philadelphia, Tom Skinner's work in New York, Jesse Jackson's Operation PUSH in Chicago, and several others.

During that year, H. came to join us. When I had first invited H., I'd said, "Man, let's go to Jackson and create another VOC." Well, by the time H. arrived we were sure—we wanted to start a new work in Jackson. Our vision for Jackson went beyond our vision for Mendenhall. From the very start we wanted the Jackson VOC to be a reconciled community, a fellowship of blacks and whites ministering to blacks and whites, drawing into its fellowship both blacks and whites. We wanted the Jackson VOC to be a reconciling community, freeing both blacks and whites from the prejudices which chained them. With a white family and a black family making up the initial leadership team we seemed to be off on the right foot.

The Jackson area had so much potential. Reformed Theological Seminary and three colleges with Christian roots were in the area. They would all benefit from a black presence on campus and be excellent laboratories of reconciliation.

In anticipation of getting a Lilly Foundation grant for the Jackson work, H. and I spent a full year in developing a detailed five-year plan for the ministry as part of our grant application. It seemed all but certain that the funding would come through. But it didn't. And that turned out to be one of the best things that happened to us. By that time H. and I were fully committed to starting the Jackson VOC. There was no question—even without the grant we would go ahead.

Almost two thousand years ago, a fellowship of believers in Antioch fasted and prayed. They then gathered around two of their own, Paul and Barnabas, laid their hands on them and sent them off into the work to which God had called them (see Acts 13:2,3). In that same spirit, one Sunday morning in the fall of 1974, our little fellowship in Mendenhall gathered around H. and me, committed us to the Lord, and sent us out into our new work.

We were off!

REFLECTION

1. What links do you see between the author's forgiving those who had wronged him, and God's empowering him to be a reconciler?
2. In what sense did the author's vision for the Jackson ministry surpass his original vision for the Mendenhall ministry?
3. What opportunities (needs) for a ministry of reconciliation can you identify in your own community?

11

THE RECONCILED COMMUNITY

To carve out of the heart of Jackson, Mississippi a community of believers reconciled to God and to each other—that was our dream. To bring together a fellowship of blacks and whites, rich and poor, who would live together, worship together and reach out together as the people of God. We believed that if we would faithfully be the people of God in our neighborhood we could make a positive difference in the lives of people enslaved by poverty and racism.

Others might have thought our dream absurd or impossible. Yet H. and I, our families, and the sending fellowship at Mendenhall dared to believe it was possible for one reason: God said so. His Word made it clear that racial reconciliation was not only possible, but mandatory for the Body of Christ. God, that night in the Brandon jail, called me to take the gospel to whites as well as blacks. And now it seemed clear to me and Vera Mae, to H. and Terry, and to the Mendenhall fellowship, that Jackson was to be our next mission field.

We wanted our church to be much more than a worshiping congregation; we wanted it to be the family of God, the Body of Christ within our community. To really function as Christ's

Body we would each have to recognize the unique spiritual gifts which each person brought to the fellowship. We would have to recognize that we could not truly operate as a Body unless we used our spiritual gifts to minister to each other, to sharpen each other. And then we would have to blend our gifts together in reaching out into the neighborhood in a way that would meet the needs of people and bring glory to Christ.

We decided that our best strategy in Jackson was to have both a church—Voice of Calvary Fellowship, and a ministry organization—Voice of Calvary Ministries. The church would be the vehicle for the relationships. The ministry organization would direct the community development programs. By keeping the two separate, people from other churches could work with us in VOCM without feeling pressured to join our church. Through VOCM we hoped to draw many pastors and congregations into the work of reconciliation and community development.

Though Mississippi might not have offered any historical precedents for a reconciled fellowship, the book of Acts did. We drew inspiration particularly from the Antioch fellowship—a church which demonstrated both the possibility and the necessity of reconciliation within the Body of Christ.

"Now there were at Antioch, in the church that was there, prophets and teachers: Barnabas, and Simeon who was called Niger, and Lucius of Cyrene, and Manaen who had been brought up with Herod the tetrarch, and Saul" (Acts 13:1). This one verse reveals a lot about the church at Antioch. The leadership team included black—Simon called Niger, and white—Gentile Lucius of Cyrene, and Jew—aristocrat Manaen, and the common man. The fellowship of Antioch transcended racial, cultural, and social barriers. Not only were these groups represented in the congregation, they were its leaders. Evidently there weren't any Jews saying, "Now you black folk come from a bad background, and what you've got to do is study and work your way up, and when you get it all together you can be a teacher." Rather, it seems the Holy Spirit spontaneously gifted those He chose and brought them together into a unified team.

Now that doesn't mean that the Antioch church was without its tensions. When the Jewish Christians first went there they preached the gospel only to Jews. It was not until Christians from Cyprus and Cyrene—evidently converted at Pentecost—came to Antioch that the gospel was preached to the Greeks (see Acts 11:19,20).

Then Peter touched off a tense situation. While he was visiting in Antioch, Jews from the circumcision party arrived. Fearing their criticism Peter quit eating with the Gentiles. Then the rest of the Jews from that local fellowship followed Peter's lead. Even Barnabas gave in to the pressure.

Paul minced no words about the seriousness of Peter's sin. He said that Peter "stood condemned" (Gal. 2:11), that his act was "hypocrisy" (v. 13) and that the Jews were not being "straightforward about the truth of the gospel" (v. 14). So severe was Peter's offense that Paul publicly rebuked him before the whole church. For the Jews to hold themselves separate from the Gentiles when God had declared them one was to violate the very truth of the gospel.

And so it is today. When blacks and whites who have worked and shopped and studied and eaten side by side all week go to segregated churches on Sunday morning at 11:00 A.M., the gospel itself is betrayed. Where I come from in Mississippi, I don't know what we assume the gospel is supposed to do. If the gospel doesn't bring you into relationship with God, then bring you into relationship with your fellowman, then make you want to bring other people into that relationship, I can't imagine what the gospel is for.

The only purpose of the gospel is to reconcile people to God and to each other. A gospel that doesn't reconcile is not a Christian gospel at all. But in America it seems as if we don't believe that. We don't really believe that the proof of our discipleship is that we love one another (see John 13:35). No, we think the proof is in numbers—church attendance, decision cards. Even if our "converts" continue to hate each other, even if they will not worship with their brothers and sisters in Christ, we point to their "conversion" as evidence of the gospel's success. We have substituted a gospel of church growth for a gospel of reconciliation.

And how convenient it is that our "church growth experts" tell us that homogenous churches grow fastest! That welcome news seems to relieve us of the responsibility to overcome racial barriers in our churches. It seems to justify not bothering with breaking down racial barriers, since that would only distract us from "church growth." And so the most segregated racist institution in America, the evangelical church, racks up the numbers, declaring itself "successful," oblivious to the fact that the dismemberment of the Body of Christ broadcasts to the world every day a hypocrisy as blatant as Peter's at Antioch—a living denial of the truth of the gospel.

Black separatism and white exclusiveness often grow out of a fear of what interracial relationships might bring. Our exclusiveness is our attempt to avoid suffering and conflict. Whenever two different groups of any kind come together, there is conflict. For that conflict to be resolved, somebody has to take the heat. The work of reconciliation calls for a leader who can draw out that hostility, who can accept that hostility himself, and who can bring together the conflicting people or groups.

Jesus, the Great Reconciler, suffered the agony of all our sins—an agony far beyond our comprehension. Yet without that suffering there would have been no reconciliation. We would still be God's enemies. If we are going to share in Christ's mission we must also share in His suffering. "For to you it has been granted for Christ's sake, not only to believe in Him, but also to suffer for His sake" (Phil. 1:29). We cannot follow Christ without taking up our crosses (see Matt. 10:38).

James says, "Consider it all joy, my brethren, when you encounter various trials; knowing that the testing of your faith produces endurance. And let endurance have its perfect result, that you may be perfect and complete, lacking in nothing" (Jas. 1:2-4). I think James needed to think of a word other than "joy" because it's not going to be joyful. But it is going to be good and it's going to be healthy. We must not try to avoid the suffering and short-circuit this process. Even when we ask for physical healing our primary motive should not be to end the suffering, but rather to be able to throw our whole bodies back into God's work again.

H. and I were under no illusion that the work in Jackson would be easy. Most blacks didn't want whites in their churches, and most whites didn't want blacks in their churches. What we were coming to establish, most people didn't want. To be reconcilers in a racist city we would have to suffer the hostility of both blacks and whites.

The duty to "bear one another's burdens" (Gal. 6:2) takes on added meaning in an interracial fellowship. When a white brother comes to the community he's bringing all his superiority and all his guilt which society has put on him. I must be able and willing to absorb that if we are to be reconciled.

And my white brother in the community must also recognize that I bring my history of being treated inferior, of being told I am a nobody, a nigger. He must understand that I am trying to claim my worth as a person created in God's image. So he must bear the burden of all my bitterness and anger that grows out of my past.

To be reconciled to each other, then, we must bear the burdens created by each other's pasts. And to be reconcilers in the world, to bring others together, we must bear the burdens of both the parties we seek to reconcile.

Since we wanted our ministry to be to both blacks and whites, we chose a target neighborhood which was about 80 percent white, and turning black. At the rate it was changing over, it would be all black in four or five years. In establishing our community there, one of our goals was to transform the neighborhood into one where blacks and whites would live together in harmony.

We bought a big house in our target area which we called the Four C Center—the Center for Continuous Christian Community. H. and Terry moved into it. The Four C Center was seven blocks from the Jackson State University campus, a black university where we wanted to establish a ministry.

From the beginning we were convinced that the ministry had to be based in Christian community. We had to be based in community because only that kind of intense interdependence—an actual sharing of our lives—could mold us into the kind of ministry team that could make a strong positive impact on our neighborhood. And we needed to be a Christian community because community would provide just the right kind of laboratory for working out the tough nitty-gritty of reconciliation.

Community is a place where people can be human beings, where they can be healed and strengthened in their deepest emotions, and where they can walk towards unity and interior freedom. As fears and prejudices diminish and trust in God and others grows, the community can radiate a witness to a style and quality of life which will bring a solution to the troubles of our world.[10]

In Jackson we did not define community, as some groups have, in terms of all living in extended households, though our community does have extended households. We outlined a geographical area of a six-block radius within which the families in our community would live. Vera Mae and I moved from our house in another part of Jackson and bought a house in our ministry area. We knew that to be effective we had to live among the people we were ministering to.

We started out by holding Bible classes in the Four C Center. Then in 1975 we started our church fellowship.

Our first community development program was People's Development, Inc. Herbert Jones, back from Maryland Bible Institute, joined us on staff in Jackson as the director of PDI. This ministry involves buying old houses, remodeling them, and selling them at reasonable rates. The starting capital for the business in Jackson came from our personal income.

Vera Mae and I decided to live on about $8,000 a year, and H. and Terry lived on about $6,000. All our income above that went to PDI. That year I earned about $10,000 from my consulting work and Terry earned about $10,000 from her work as a nurse at the hospital; all that went into this fund. We borrowed another $30,000 and started buying houses. These houses provided homes within our target area for people joining our community.

Worshiping in a house posed a problem: Black people don't like to go to church in a house. They like to go to a church building. So we started focusing our ministry on the kids, hoping to reach the parents through them. Our ministry started bearing fruit and people from the community started coming to our church.

Our success, though, created a problem. People outside

our community began to come to our church too. Now we wanted people to join us in our ministry, but we also wanted our church to be much more than a place where we worshiped together. We wanted it to be a Christian community—a team of Christians deeply committed to God and each other and to a common task—reaching our neighborhood with a holistic gospel. We had a unique purpose—to serve the people who lived in our target area.

One evening we met at our house with all the people attending our fellowship. I encouraged everyone who did not live in our target community to join churches in their own neighborhoods. We were convinced that people who did not live in the target area could not really bear the burdens of those who did. They would not have the same kind of concern for the target community as those who lived there and whose children went to school there.

Several of these families, then, moved into our community. Some, of course, stayed where they were and found churches in their own neighborhoods. This decision, I believe, was crucial to our effectiveness in the neighborhood.

As the church grew we created what we call household groups. These small groups met once a week for Bible study and sharing. Ideally we wanted these household groups to consist of people from the same neighborhood who would get to know each other by eating and playing and studying and praying together. This shared life, then, would strengthen their witness in their neighborhoods. Like most churches we have a choir, Sunday School, prayer meeting, and so on, but our main life together is in the household groups.

Ten elders lead our fellowship. They take turns speaking, they lead the household groups, and together they make decisions about the life of our fellowship. One of our elders, Phil Reed, serves as our pastor. He is responsible to see that the decisions of the elders are carried out.

We generally make our decisions by consensus, not by voting. For example, when we chose Phil as our pastor we didn't vote. We prayed, seeking God's direction for whom we should choose. Someone suggested that we make Phil our pastor, and it seemed right to the rest of us.

The elders take turns moderating the elders' meetings. The

moderator leads the discussion and determines when a decision has been reached. Of course, the elders don't make all the decisions; any major decisions are made by the congregation as a whole.

All these things—living close together, meeting in household groups, making decisions by consensus, rotating moderators—help to nurture community. But these structures are not in themselves Christian community. Christian community is personal relationships. It is people loving each other. And no matter how perfectly we plan the community structure or procedures, as long as people are human, achieving and maintaining unity will never be easy. We rediscovered this fact when we began to build our community in Jackson.

REFLECTION
1. Do you agree that "a gospel that doesn't reconcile is not a Christian gospel at all"? What does that mean?
2. If reconciliation is at the very heart of the gospel, what is the church's responsibility where groups of people are divided by racial, cultural, social, or economic barriers? How important a part of the church's mission is it to tear down these barriers?
3. What does the author mean by "Christian community"? Why did he feel it was essential for the Jackson ministry to be rooted in a Christain community?
4. What are some of the structures which help to nurture community in the Jackson fellowship? How do you feel each structure contributes to community?
5. What is a reconciled Christian community?

12

THE ROCKY ROAD TO RECONCILIATION

The benediction brought the service to a close. The chapel speaker, Dr. Richard Williams, a longtime friend of mine from Tampa, Florida, began to make his way off the platform. As was the custom, he and I were invited to the faculty lounge to meet informally with the faculty for a few minutes before the next class period. But the seminary students crowded around us, eager to talk.

We finally made it into the faculty lounge only to be greeted by a mass exodus of professors hurrying off to their classes. All, that is, except one. He introduced himself—Dr. Paul Fowler, assistant professor of New Testament there at Reformed Theological Seminary in Jackson. He had just moved to Jackson from rural Georgia where he pastored. We talked for a while and decided to get together again. Only later did he tell me why he skipped class that day. He was afraid I would think the faculty were all leaving because a black person walked in, when actually they were leaving to get to class on time.

Well, Paul and I began to dream together. I began to share my vision of what could happen in Jackson if we, whites and blacks, could be reconciled to each other—if we could join hands in reaching out to the city.

Paul got excited. We began eating lunch together once a month to discuss reconciliation. Pretty soon, Paul invited nine other Presbyterian ministers to meet with us—Phil Esty, the late Carlos Smith, Cobbe Ware, Lanier Ellis, Sam Patterson, Jim McGuire, David Ray, Gary Spooner, and Bill Lowery.

Reverend Phil Esty, pastor of the Covenant Presbyterian Church in Jackson, was so eager to help that two months later he brought the leading men of his congregation together for me to speak to them. He hoped that this meeting might spark a combined effort of outreach into Jackson, a reconciled witness to the city. I had high hopes. Here a white congregation was reaching out to join us as reconciled partners.

That night I took along the guys from Mendenhall and some men from the North who were visiting with us. That proved to be a mistake. As we shared, the meeting turned into a confrontation. At the close of the meeting Phil stood and told how disappointed he was. My heart was broken. Our brightest flicker of hope for reconciliation in Jackson—snuffed out.

That night, with Paul Fowler along, we went back to our friends' hotel room and prayed and wept together. We had so wanted God to bless our relationship with this church, and now there seemed to be no chance. In the valley of that disheartening failure I reaffirmed to God my commitment to a ministry of reconciliation. So did Paul. And wherever Phil was that night he must have been doing the same thing, because he never gave up on us. Within a few months he had me back to speak in his church. He invited our choir over to sing. Today Phil serves on the board of Thriftco, one of our business organizations, and his church is one of VOC's strongest supporters. Out of that stormy beginning God brought real reconciliation.

Some of our attempts at reconciliation didn't end quite so well. In the following months I spoke twice at Reformed Theological Seminary. What I was saying about reconciliation and a holistic gospel was new to a lot of students and drew excited responses—some positive, some negative.

One student there was a member of a church in the delta area. He and his wife started attending our fellowship regularly. He was eager for racial reconciliation but overly concerned about our statement of faith. He was always wanting to defend his doctrinal beliefs and be sure we agreed with him. When he would ask me about our statement of faith I would assure him that we knew what we believed, we had a statement in our file cabinet, but we were more concerned with living out our beliefs than we were with defending their correctness. That is still true today. In fact, it was not until four years ago, after we had thoroughly worked through our statement of *purpose*—what real evangelism is, the importance of reconciliation, justice, and so on—that we began to print our statement of *faith* in our publications.

Well, one Sunday this seminary student preached at VOCF, and his wife played the organ. Then they just disappeared. We have never seen them since.

An important step forward in black and white Christians ministering together in Mississippi came in 1975 with the Mississippi Billy Graham Crusade. Several months before the crusade the steering committee met at the Holiday Inn on I-55 on the north side of town. As we gathered, the very fact that black and white pastors were meeting together created an atmosphere of jubilation.

The meeting was well on its way when I threw a bug into the punch. I stood up and said, "I really appreciate Billy Graham's stand in refusing to bring a crusade to an area unless the races and denominations cooperate. But I'm not sure I want to work to make any more of the same kind of white Christians we've had in the past.

"You see, I want to invite as many unsaved blacks to the crusade as I can. When they come, they're going to see me sitting on the platform and think, 'This must be okay.' When Dr. Graham gives the invitation many of them are going to respond and give their lives to Christ. Then some of them are going to want to come to your churches, and do you know what's going to happen? You're going to turn them away! I don't want to destroy the credibility of my years of work for justice because I identify with that kind of religion."

Some of those white pastors really heard me. They came up to me after the meeting to say they agreed with what I had said. For some reason, though, the black preachers didn't seem that pleased. They seemed to think I had raised an issue that should have been left alone. Things like this make me wonder if black pastors really want blacks and whites to worship together. It often seems that, for whatever reasons, they want to stay separate as much as the whites do.

Well, of course, my predictions about the Billy Graham Crusade came true. But it was still a breakthrough for black-white cooperation.

Our goal in Jackson was to build bridges wherever we could. We invited businessmen and pastors to monthly luncheons to tell them about new ministry projects. Occasionally H., I and other members of our staff attended Christian Businessmen's luncheons.

Faith at Work has also been an effective bridge-builder, breaking down racial and denominational barriers. The first Faith at Work Conference came to the state in 1975. Faith at Work holds interdenominational weekend retreats that focus on developing personal relationships, especially through small sharing groups. People really get to know each other as people. Many of these relationships, including new friendships between blacks and whites, continue long after the retreats.

In '76 we staged what we called a Day of Reconciliation. We brought together about 25 black leaders and about 25 white leaders from Jackson and Mendenhall. Several of us shared our own testimonies of our own experiences of prejudice in the past, where God had brought us, and our vision for future reconciliation.

H. helped to get the first black chapter of Inter-Varsity Christian Fellowship started on the Jackson State campus, a predominantly black campus with about 8,000 students. Campus Crusade also started a work at Jackson State. Their two black staff members joined our fellowship and we helped to support them.

Vera got involved in several predominantly white Christian groups, such as Christian Women's Club, and the Explorer's Bible Class taught by Jeanne Patterson, the pastor's wife from First Presbyterian Church, one of the leading missionary churches in the country.

I was building relationships with the colleges in the area

too. In addition to getting to know many of the Jackson State faculty I was getting to speak at Belhaven College, a predominantly white Presbyterian college with about 1,000 students, and Millsaps College, a Methodist school of about 1,200 students.

Everywhere we went we took the same message: we must be reconciled to both God and man.

The gospel's first work is to reconcile us to God: "God . . . reconciled us to Himself through Christ" (2 Cor. 5:18). Then if our relationship with God is right it will show up in our relationships with each other: "If some one says, 'I love God,' and hates his brother, he is a liar; for the one who does not love his brother whom he has seen, cannot love God whom he has not seen" (1 John 4:20).

For my worship to be acceptable to God, I must be reconciled to my brother: "If therefore you are presenting your offering at the altar, and there remember that your brother has something against you, leave your offering there before the altar, and go your way; first be reconciled to your brother, and then come and present your offering" (Matt. 5:23,24).

To be reconciled to my brother I must first be reconciled to God; to remain reconciled to God I must be reconciled to my brother. I cannot have one without the other.

As the Jackson ministry grew we moved VOC's headquarters from Mendenhall to Jackson. This meant that our Jackson headquarters was subsidizing the work in Mendenhall. Our goal was that the Mendenhall ministry would one day be self-sufficient. One way we hoped to make that possible was through our thrift store.

Well, in the summer of 1978, while we were at Cedine Camp, I was reviewing our leadership development program. I thought of my son Spencer, my daughter Joanie, Sarah and Eva Quinn, Lynn Phillips, and Marlene Hardy—all young folks from Mendenhall who were attending college and working on our staff in Jackson. I realized they had become too dependent on the Voice of Calvary Ministries. Because we had guaranteed them all jobs they had never yet had to find jobs on their own. They had never gotten any work experience out "in the real world." So I decided we needed to take them off staff. They needed to go away, get some experience, develop some independence, then come back and work with us.

That decision prompted me to reevaluate where we stood with the Mendenhall ministry. Artis was pastoring the church, Dolphus directing the ministry. I began to feel like that ministry had become too dependent, just as the young staff in Jackson had become too dependent. I would cut off the Mendenhall ministry from our support, I decided, and work out a way for the staff to raise their own support.

I decided that on my own. Although VOCM had just established a board of directors which we call our Board of Servants, I didn't consult them. I didn't consult with anyone. I just wrote Artis and Dolphus a short letter telling them that after three months they would be on their own; they would have to raise their own support.

They were stunned. And hurt. A rift grew between us. I started getting letters and phone calls from people who loved both ministries who were upset because of what Dolphus and Artis had told them I had done.

I retaliated. I figured that if they wanted to make an issue of it I could fight right back. For months a spirit of competition divided us. Members of our Board of Servants and staff members tried to bring reconciliation between us, but I told them not to get involved.

I justified my attitude toward Dolphus and Artis on the grounds that I had a father-son relationship with them, and that they had to be put in their places in order to become men. They had to take responsibility for the ministry themselves. If they wanted to rebel against me that was okay. That was part of what a father was for.

One night, after I had spoken in a church in South Dakota, I got in bed and couldn't sleep. I couldn't sleep because I didn't feel my heart was right with God or with them. Here I was, the person so big on reconciliation, in need of reconciliation myself. So I had to get on the phone right then and ask them to forgive me. Then I wrote both of them a letter. When I came home we met together and talked it through.

To Artis and Dolphus, my cutting them off had felt like a personal rejection. Of course I hadn't meant it that way. I was trying to help the ministry stand on its own two feet. I still feel like the goal was right. Dolphus and Artis have since taken responsibility for their own finances and the Mendenhall ministry has become strong and independent. What was wrong was the way I went about it. I still don't know how else I could have achieved the same goals. I do know, though, that I should have consulted with other people—Dolphus, Artis, the Board of Servants, the VOCM management team. It is out of a multitude of counsel that good decisions come.

But I didn't do that. And the broken and strained relationships that resulted from acting alone made me realize all the more what I knew in my head already—in a Christian community changes must not be based on one-man decisions; they must grow out of the decision of the Body.

From time to time I still ask Artis and Dolphus to forgive me. I think that's because the hurt I caused them still isn't completely healed. That is a grief I just have to live with.

I also think of those days in Mendenhall when I was working for liberty and justice for our people. I hadn't yet seen how the white people in Mendenhall were victims of their own society. I didn't yet see them through eyes of compassion. I saw their faults but not their needs. And so my work for justice was motivated by a tempered hostility rather than by love and a passion for reconciliation. With that kind of motive I must have unintentionally hurt some of those white people too, though I don't know whom I hurt or how. I want to ask those white folks I hurt to forgive me.

Reconciliation is never easy. It requires humbling yourself to say, "I'm sorry." It means forgiving. It's a tough, often painful struggle. But it's the kind of struggle worth being in.

The fruits of our work for reconciliation are not always easy to measure. There sometimes seem to more setbacks than successes. But sometimes something happens that reassures us that it is working, that it is worth it.

In 1977, blacks and whites in New Hebron, our hometown, got together and asked VOC to establish a health center. They had been without a doctor for 12 years. So H. went down and helped to get that health center going. Around that health center has developed another little VOC community of blacks and whites who have joined the Oak Ridge Baptist Church there in New Hebron—the church Vera Mae and I worked in when we first came back to Mississippi.

One of the outreaches of our Health Center in New Hebron is a child evangelism program, directed by Mrs. Annie Bell Young. Through it many of the children are coming to know Christ. These black Christian children coming to our Bible classes started talking about Jesus at school. Some of the white Christian teachers responded to that. So the kids asked the white teachers where they were learning about the Bible. They answered that it was at their church. One of the black kids then asked, "Can we go to your church?"

Well, they couldn't go to their church. No blacks were allowed there. The teachers felt convicted about this and decided to find a way to reach more kids with the gospel. They hit on the idea of having an evangelistic crusade in the school football stadium. They scheduled the evangelist, a white pastor from the county Baptist association, then decided to hold prayer meetings to prepare for the crusade.

Where could they hold the prayer meetings? Our staff invited them to join us at the health center for our weekly prayer meeting, and they did. The new pastor of the First Baptist Church started coming to these meetings and got caught up in the project.

Next they decided that they needed to train black counselors for the crusade. Where could they hold the training? It was all right to hold a prayer meeting at the health center from seven to eight in the morning, but training counselors would take more than an hour or two. Well, that new pastor decided to open up his church's educational unit for the training—the first time blacks had ever been allowed in the church building. More was probably accomplished in the relationships formed in preparing for the crusade than through the crusade itself!

Brother Eugene Walker who was telling us this story summed it up like this: "Well, Voice of Calvary has done a lot for us. It helped us get Bible classes going. It helped us get economic development going. It helped us get our kids through college. It helped us with our farm. It helped us with voter registration. It brought us a health clinic. And now the last thing it's been able to do is to integrate the church."

The last thing! How tragic, when reconciliation should begin, not end, with the church. Yet that it has happened at all is one more sign of hope.

The road to reconciliation is never easy. Yet it is a road we must travel. The gospel demands it.

The walls may not be crashing down as they did at Jericho, but at least I can see them beginning to crumble.

God *is* bringing us together.

REFLECTION

1. As the author's experience illustrates, we who are called to be reconcilers will from time to time find ourselves in need of reconciliation. Why is it often hard to be reconciled to a brother or sister? What will result if we do not become reconciled?

2. What kind of person does it take to be a reconciler?

3. Between what two groups of people in your community is there the greatest need for reconciliation?

4. Using the examples from this chapter to stimulate ideas, list eight or ten things that churches or individuals might do to build bridges between these two groups. Think of key people, key groups with whom bridges would need to be built.

5. What barriers or opposition would you expect any such efforts at reconciliation to encounter?

13

TEN YEARS LATER

Ten years later to the day after that night of horrors in the Brandon jail, February 7, 1980, I found myself standing on the platform with the governor of Mississippi being honored as the state's outstanding religious leader of the year. What a remarkable testimony of God's healing grace!

Later that same year in Wheaton, Illinois, Wheaton College awarded me—a third grade dropout—an honorary Doctor of Law degree in recognition of my work in Mississippi. What a tribute to God's ability to perfect His power in weakness!

When I'm in the middle of the work it often seems like our progress is painfully slow, but when I step back and look at all that God has brought into being through Voice of Calvary in these 22 years, it amazes me. I'd like to show you how far God has brought us.

I'd like to take you, first of all, on a tour of Mendenhall.

As we come into Mendenhall on old highway 49, we turn south and cross over the tracks into the quarters. On your right is a beautiful brick building housing our first major economic enterprise—the Thrift Store. The Thrift Store sells all kinds of new and used merchandise—gardening supplies,

hardware, clothing, even food from our farm. This store has one of the biggest volumes of retail sales in town. Even though it is located in the black community, 60 to 65 percent of our customers are white, and we employ both blacks and whites from the community.

Let me tell you how we started this store. Years back people were giving things, both used and new, to VOC. A lot of it we couldn't use. So we just gave it away. Well, some people started taking more than they needed and setting up their own distribution spots. So we started holding rummage sales two Saturdays a month in our gym. That worked out so well that we decided to see if we could run a thrift store. So for two years we had this store in an old funeral home. It was such a success that we built this modern $250,000 store building right here between the black and white parts of town.

T. J. Moore, a black man from the community, manages the store. Dolphus projects that within three years the store will reach its goal of being able to channel profits back into the community through the holistic ministries of the church.

As we come on down into the quarters we turn south on Center Street. We've come now to the Voice of Calvary complex. These two houses on the corner are ours. And this big building here on the east side of the street houses Genesis One—our preschool—and the Legal Services.

As I mentioned before, Genesis One was started by two volunteers from Wheaton. Judy Adams, our doctor's wife, has led it ever since. This year Genesis has about 30 students, ages four to six, with 15 or 20 children on the waiting list. Students pay 10 to 15 dollars per week, which covers 60 percent of the cost per child. The other 40 percent is raised through community fundraising and the church. On the tests students take when they enter the public school, our Genesis students have scored higher than most preschoolers.

Genesis is a good example of how the felt need concept has worked. Several of our college educated staff in Mendenhall, such as Dennis and Judy Adams, Dolphus and Rosie, and Artis and Carolyn, have young children. They want those children to have good educational opportunities so they are willing to do what it takes to make the school work. Because the community's needs are their needs, they are offering a service

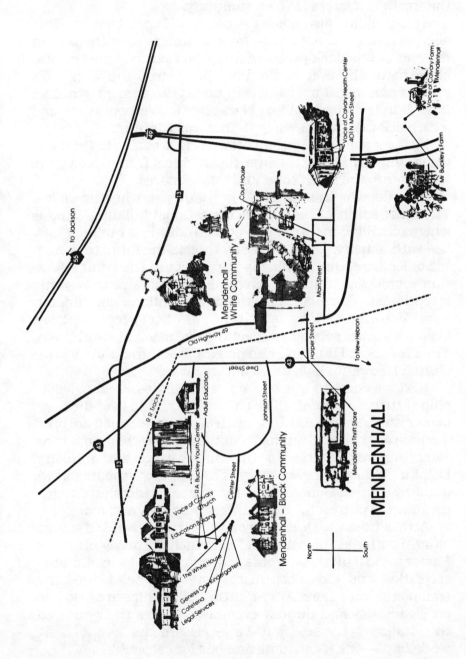

that really ministers to the community.

This building also holds the offices of Legal Services. This also grew out of a felt need—my encounters with the law. In the eyes of the black people of Simpson County, I am the first black man who ever confronted the system and won. Now some people might not call a compromise settlement winning, but I didn't end up in jail and I was free to keep working—and for a black man in Mississippi, that was winning.

Now, for the first time, an attorney is available to the black community. And, for the first time, whites from uptown are coming into the black community for services.

Next door to this building is the house where we lived. Then just south of that is our educational building. This is where our Bible Institute was born. Today this building bustles with activity. Dolphus Weary directs the ministries from his office here. Judy Williams, a product of the adult education secretarial training, serves as Dolphus's secretary and receptionist. Glynnis Polk is communications coordinator. Vera Johnson works part-time as bookkeeper. Rosie, Dolphus's wife, schedules speaking engagements and travel. The educational building also houses the church nursery, the church fellowship hall, and a library.

Next we come to our church sanctuary where our fellowship gathers to worship. The church fellowship is at the heart of everything we do. All our ministries in Mendenhall are operated through the church. Pastor Artis Fletcher and three elders are responsible for the church's life and ministry. Dolphus Weary is the ministry administrator responsible for adult education, Genesis One, recreation, leadership development, radio outreach, the volunteer program, and more.

Across from the sanctuary on the corner is our big gymnasium. Youth meetings are held here each Saturday night. On Monday and Thursday nights the gym opens for community recreation and kids flock in to play basketball, Ping-Pong, trampoline, and more. After-meeting fellowships are held here on Wednesday and Sunday evenings. Besides the gym itself, this building houses four large classrooms and two big workshops—one for welding and one for carpentry.

Next to the gym sits a yellow brick building which once housed our first cooperative venture—a general store. During the sixties it was the home of the NAACP and hosted various civil rights gatherings. Today it is an adult education center where on Mondays and Thursdays over 40 adults study math, history, typing, sewing, welding, and other subjects which lead to high school diplomas and employment.

Though we helped to start the adult education program and our staff are actively involved in it, it is not actually run by VOC. The program is conducted by Co-Lin Junior College and staffed by qualified local teachers. The building is owned by the Civic League, an organization we helped to start back in the sixties in the voter registration drive days.

That's the end of the VOC complex itself. But a few blocks north we come to our two-acre playground. This is still the only playground in the black community of Mendenhall.

As you look around you'll still see a lot of the same shacks that we found when we moved to Mendenhall 21 years ago. But also, interspersed among the shacks, are many nice houses. Some of them are new. A lot have been remodeled. Many of these nice homes are the direct or indirect result of the Simpson County Development Project. This housing co-op was our response to the pitiful housing in Mendenhall. We found out that Farmers Home Administration had long-term loans available at three percent interest. At first we didn't have a black FHA representative in our area. But after enough letters to Washington and Jackson, they finally sent us a man, Mr. Alexander, just to work primarily with us on this project. The project built about 10 units, and several families were able to get FHA loans on their own because Mr. Alexander was here to work with them. Before this, most of the people in the community didn't even see the need for better housing. Our housing project kind of started the ball rolling. People could see that better housing was possible and, those who could, started doing something about it.

I have one more building to show you. The Voice of Calvary Health Center in Mendenhall used to be in what is now the Legal Services building, but in '74 a flood wiped it out. It did $8,500 worth of damage to our new X-ray machine alone, which we were going to dedicate that very evening. So we began praying for a clinic location above the flood plain.

God answered that prayer far beyond our expectation by

enabling us to buy a clinic in the best location in town, right across from the courthouse. Our clinic is the only black-owned piece of property in the white part of town.

If we were to walk inside we would see blacks and whites seated together in the same waiting room. Dennis Adams, a black doctor, sees about 35 patients a day. Pediatric nurse practitioner Vera Schertz, Jeannie Visnovsky, a nutritionist, and Elsie Lee, LPN, assist Dr. Adams. Peggie Harrington, RN, operates the WIC (Women, Infants, and Children) program.

Not only is our health center providing excellent health care to the blacks in Simpson County for the first time; it has also inspired several of our young people to go into health-related professions.

From here I want to take you a few miles northeast of town to our cooperative farm. Way back in the first days of VOC, Mr. Buckley started letting us use his farm to raise food for the VOC family and for feeding the children in our tutoring program. The one meal a day we fed these children was often all that stood between them and malnutrition.

Well, today VOC owns land right next to Mr. Buckley's so that all together we have about 240 acres to farm. A white family, Don and Joanne Mansfields, and a black family, Fred and Penny Shaw, manage the farm. They have about 40 acres in crops—strawberries, okra, cabbage, turnips, cucumbers, watermelon, peas, potatoes, corn, peanuts, greens, beans, and fruit trees; the rest is pasture. They have 30 head of beef, 27 feeder pigs, and a chicken farm that produces 45 dozen eggs a week.

In addition to providing food, the farm provides a good place for our young people to work. When they see their leaders with graduate degrees coming out to the farm to chop in the fields they see that there is dignity in physical labor.

Our newest cooperative in Mendenhall is the Automotive Service Cooperative, an auto repair shop located on the highway northeast of town.

That wraps up the Mendenhall ministry. It's a strong ministry, financially independent, led by indigenous leaders— people who grew up in this community, rose through our leadership development program, went off to school, then returned to take over the work. That's what needs to be happening in every poor community across our country.

Now let's go to Jackson. Let's begin our tour here at 1655 St. Charles Street, the VOC Fellowship House. This is the first house we bought in Jackson, our original Four C Center. We use it for everything. For years our fellowship worshiped here. When we outgrew this house church, we rented a church building on Lynch Street for a year. We now rent the Masonic Temple in the same neighborhood.

Behind the fellowship house is an old milk dairy which we've turned into offices. From offices in these two buildings president Lem Tucker directs Voice of Calvary Ministries, assisted by Timothy Whitehead; Donna Wheeler serves as office manager; Debbie Taylor heads up development; Richard Clark supervises the accounting department; Joan Perkins oversees communications; and Don Strohnbehn directs PDI. Capable staff assist in every area of the work.

At noon, staff and volunteers converge on the fellowship house's big lunchroom, where we fellowship over our meal together.

Just across the street and around the corner is our Herbert R. Jones Christian Youth Center which we now use for our Child Evangelism Fellowship ministry. Evangelism is definitely our top ministry priority. In addition to CEF, we reach out evangelistically through Bible classes, Campus Crusade, Inter-Varsity, and tent meetings.

In the neighborhood around the fellowship house you see quite a few houses that PDI has remodeled. People's Development, Inc. is a nonprofit housing cooperative which stimulates neighborhood revitalization by purchasing and renovating deteriorating homes. Established in 1974, PDI now owns 14 homes within this 20-square block area in West Jackson. The neighborhood people appreciate the constant improvement of neighborhood homes PDI stimulates. PDI provides home ownership to people who would otherwise be unable to afford it and this encourages other homeowners to maintain and improve their homes. Staff members conduct weatherization seminars to help local residents creatively cope with rising energy costs. PDI not only meets housing needs but also provides summer jobs for neighborhood youth, and gives our young men valuable on-the-job training in construction skills.

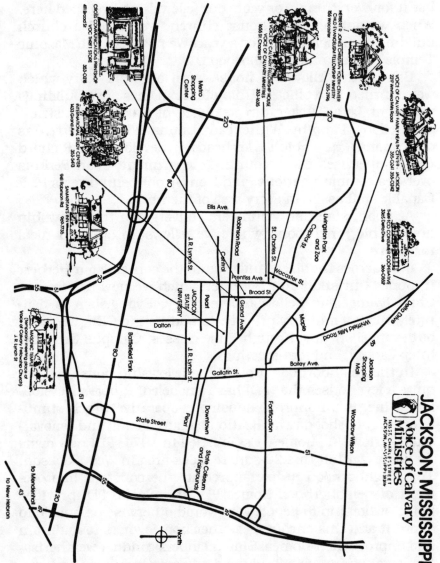

JACKSON, MISSISSIPPI

Voice of Calvary Ministries

1655 ST. CHARLES STREET
JACKSON, MISSISSIPPI 39209

James Taylor is PDI's financial coordinator.

Also in this neighborhood is Harambee House. Harambee is a Swahili word meaning "let's get together and push." This grew out of a discipling program at our church called Dinner and Discipleship. Adults from the church are paired with young people from the community who come to their homes once a week for dinner and 30-minute Bible study.

Some of these guys whom my son Derek was discipling needed a place to stay, so they ended up moving in with him. We purchased this house where Derek and Don Strohnbehn live as house dads with four teenage guys—all new Christians from poor home situations. These guys all work in some part of VOC's ministry as part of their leadership development training. Harambee House has now become a hub of activity for teens in our community.

Our print shop is called Cross Communications. This simply grew out of our own need for printing. It is set up as a separate business so that VOCM pays the print shop for its printing; the shop also does printing for other businesses. The manager, Alvin Bensen, has also developed a related public relations business. Our youngest son, Wayne, now 19, works for Al at the print shop.

Voice of Calvary has a vision for ministry beyond our own community. We believe that the community development strategy which is working in Mendenhall and Jackson and New Hebron can work throughout the country and in third-world countries. We welcome future community developers to come to Voice of Calvary to work with us and study with us to learn how to go back to their own communities and apply what they have learned. This is the purpose of the John M. Perkins International Study Center, headed by Tim Robertson. This two-story, 15-room house includes a classroom, a library, study rooms, and living quarters for up to 12 students. Our goal is to have 12 full-time students each year, in addition to the short-term volunteers who are also trained at the ISC.

A ways east of the study center is our Samaritan's Inn. This spacious, seven-bedroom house provides a temporary home for families who don't have a place to live. Right now we use it for volunteer housing in the summer, but eventually we hope to be able to use it year-round for homeless families.

Someone brought us a family whose car had broken down on their way from Iowa to Florida. The man and his wife, their seven-year-old daughter, and the wife's sister all ended up staying at the Samaritan's Inn for a year. All three adults became Christians. The man got a job and moved his family into an apartment. He enrolled in a seminary. Now he is on staff at a church in Florida. They finally made it to Florida— two and a half years "late."

Now come northeast with me to the largest black community in the city—Georgetown. This neighborhood around Whitfield Mills Road is a broken neighborhood, congested with rundown shotgun houses, abandoned storefronts, and overcrowded streets. Fifty-five percent of the families live below poverty level.

Right in the middle of this neighborhood, on its busiest street, sits a 4,000-square-foot brick building. VOC has bought and remodeled this old boarding house and transformed it into a source of hope for the people in the neighborhood—the Voice of Calvary Family Health Center.

The health center is equipped with four exam rooms, an X-ray room, laboratory and treatment rooms, and a pastoral counseling office. It is staffed by Dr. Herbert Myers, and nurses Loraine Hess and Kathy Fodor, both Church of the Brethren volunteers. We are adding a pharmacy which will stock the less costly generic drugs and be staffed by pharmacist Susan Bergdale.

Though VOCFHC is not a free service clinic, administrator David Woodland's primary goal is to serve people who cannot afford private doctors. Opened in 1980, this facility serves as a base of outreach into the Georgetown neighborhood. We use the back lot to host Bible classes for children and evangelistic tent meetings. Here, as throughout VOC's history, social action and evangelism go hand in hand.

Just a few blocks north of our health center is our Jackson Thrift Store. It got started much like our Mendenhall store— with rummage sales of our overflow from Mendenhall. We formed a co-op and bought a building, remodeled it, and opened the store. We recently built a large warehouse and recycling center behind the retail store. This is the only new

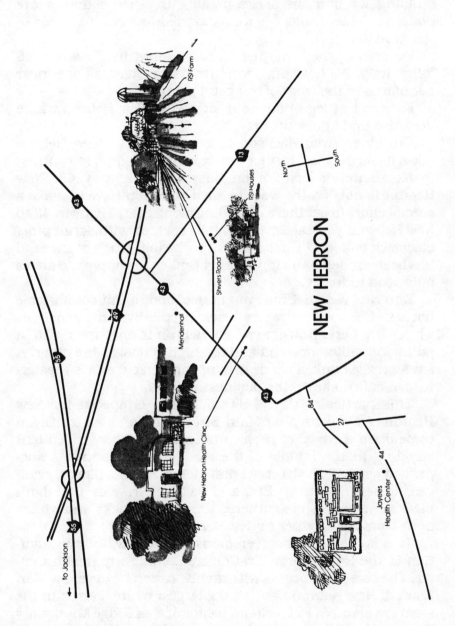

building we built in Jackson. All our other activities are housed in older buildings we remodeled to meet the needs of our ministry.

We also opened another Thriftco store in Edwards, 25 miles away. We have one more thrift store, a small one, near our offices in the front of our print shop.

For the last leg of our tour let's go to New Hebron where Vera Mae and I grew up.

Our drive from Jackson to Mendenhall to New Hebron takes us farther and farther into rural Mississippi. In contrast to Mendenhall's location on busy U.S. Highway 49, New Hebron is not "on the way" to anywhere; you have to make a special effort to get there. Traveling along State Highway 43 to New Hebron, you ease over low hills covered with scrub pine, blackjack oak, and small fields of soybeans. Much of the land has been eroded or stripped of its timber to supply the area's pulpwood industry.

Entering New Hebron, you notice modest but comfortable houses. No poor people or black people live in town; only whites live here. Downtown New Hebron is one street, with a pulpwood mill at one end and the high school at the other. A few stores, a bank, a car dealership, and an old movie-theater-turned-cafe make up the business district.

This particular day, July 26, 1981, is special for New Hebron. As you turn off Main Street onto a side street, you come upon a crowd of people under a big yellow-striped tent standing in the middle of the road; a large banner is suspended across the street. At first glance it looks like an evangelistic tent meeting. But a closer look reveals that both blacks and whites are gathered there, and blacks and whites don't worship together in New Hebron.

This is the dedication ceremony for the new building addition to the New Hebron Tri-County Community Health Center. The ceremony begins with an invocation by Reverend Earl Clark of New Hebron Baptist, the largest white church in the area. Reverend A. E. Durham, pastor of Oak Ridge Missionary Baptist, Vera Mae's home church, gives the dedication prayer.

This day symbolizes the quiet but hopeful ministry of development and reconciliation that is working in New Hebron. The door for this opened in 1978 when two groups of citizens, one white and one black, asked for my help in establishing a health clinic in New Hebron. Each group contacted me without knowledge of the other. But both knew of the critical need for better health care in their community, and both knew of the success of the Voice of Calvary clinic in Mendenhall.

It was a milestone that the white citizens of New Hebron had sought the help of a black leader in their time of need. And it was a milestone that these white and black citizens came together to improve local health care.

The clinic began operating with dental services in May 1979 and added medical services five months later. The rapidly growing practice soon demanded more space. Using an innovative five percent loan program cosponsored by the Department of Health and Human Services and the Farmers Home Administration, a new building addition was completed in February, 1981. This day's dedication ceremony celebrates the hard work that went into that building.

As the ceremony ends, the ribbon is cut and the people of the community file in to see their health center. Most of the staff and nurses who greet them are local. All three physicians, Dr. Scott Neff, Dr. Duane Claassen, and Dr. Earl Martin, and the dentist, Dr. Reid Stempel, left their homes in other parts of the country to come to Mississippi. All felt God's strong calling to use their talents and skills among the poor. All are now providing quality health care in a community which only a few years ago faced a critical shortage of health services. Also included in the work of the health center is a health education program and a nutrition center. In only a few months a new satellite clinic in the Jayess community will begin receiving patients under the team care of family nurse practitioner Irene Schomus and Dr. Earl Martin. Located 35 miles south of New Hebron and notably poor, Jayess has never had a doctor.

Unlike Voice of Calvary's work in Mendenhall and Jackson, health care was the first ministry in New Hebron. In providing health care, however, we were soon confronted with other needs which contributed to poor health, such as poor housing and unsanitary conditions. This awareness led to a broader response to the community. Health center staff supported local leaders in beginning to minister holistically to these needs.

Many of these local church leaders are in today's crowd at the dedication ceremony. Mr. Charles Hatten, chairman of the health center board and a deacon in the Oak Ridge Baptist Church, directs the Farm Project. With the help of Voice of Calvary Rural Services, Mr. Hatten is teaching agricultural skills to area farmers and local youth, demonstrating the potential profitability of family farming. Through the farm work, Mr. Hatten also disciples his young workers in the gospel.

Mr. Eugene Walker, a local black farmer and contractor, is also a deacon at the Oak Ridge Baptist Church. For years Mr. Walker has worked to improve the living conditions of poor families by renovating homes. Rural Services is now helping Mr. Walker continue this ministry.

Mrs. Annie Belle Young is a leader in the North Pleasant Hill Missionary Baptist Church. Several years ago Vera Mae challenged her to minister to the youth of her area. After attending Child Evangelism training with my wife, Mrs. Young began to set up Child Evangelism meetings in her community. With the help of Rural Services, her work has grown into a strong cooperative effort among six black churches.

Because New Hebron is different from both Mendenhall and Jackson in its character and its needs, it has called for a unique relationship between the ministry and the local church. Unlike Voice of Calvary in Mendenhall, the holistic ministry in New Hebron is not part of an official church organization. Unlike Jackson, it is not based in a strictly "Christian" organization like VOCM. However, the ministry is not independent of the church; it takes place in cooperation with, within, and through the church in the community.

The staff and volunteers relocating in New Hebron have formed a nurturing, sustaining fellowship, yet one that does not act as a church unto itself or rival the local churches around it. Through the "body life" meetings each Thursday evening, the staff and their families, along with others from the community, work out their common call to be the Body of Christ in this place.

The members of the fellowship worship at several local

black and white churches. Although black staff members cannot attend worship among white congregations, most white staff members alternate between black and white churches. The New Hebron workers enjoy a rich sense of unity with the people to whom they have submitted their skills and resources.

As I reflect on all that God has done in Mendenhall, Jackson, and New Hebron, one incident seems to symbolize His work of reconciliation. When we bought the health center building in Mendenhall, it, like every other clinic, had two entrances and two waiting rooms. The late Dr. Rotenberry, who previously operated the clinic, showed more respect for blacks than many white doctors had. Since the building was on a corner, both entrances were front entrances. And although the white entrance was nicer than the black entrance, both waiting rooms were pleasant and comfortable.

When we remodeled the building, it was a real joy to go into that waiting room with hammers and crowbars and literally tear down that dividing wall between blacks and whites. That simple act dramatically proclaimed the victory of reconciliation Jesus Christ won almost two thousand years ago: "For He Himself is our peace, who made both groups into one, and broke down the barrier of the dividing wall" (Eph. 2:14).

REFLECTION

1. What is the one needy neighborhood or community you know the most about? Close your eyes and imagine yourself walking up and down the streets of that community. What needs do you see? List them.
2. Now, drawing on the inspiration of what God has done at VOC, imagine what ministries could be in place in that neighborhood 10 years from now—ministries growing out of the needs you have seen in that community. What reconciliation could take place during the next 10 years?
3. Imagine that those 10 years have passed and your dreams are now reality. The time has come for you to write your own "Ten Years Later" account. Sketch out a brief outline of what you would include in your report. You might even include a tour of the neighborhood like one of the tours in this chapter.

14

RECONCILIATION: A STRATEGY FOR HERE AND NOW

If the purpose of the gospel is to reconcile us to God and to our fellowman, if our mission is to be God's ambassadors of reconciliation (see 2 Cor. 5:20), how do we fulfill that mission?

It's tempting for us to start out with a list of things to do. But that is not how the work of reconciliation begins. Before we can *do* the work of God, we must *be* the people of God—the believing fellowship, the Body of Christ. We cannot achieve Christ's mission each working alone; we must work as a Body, each one exercising his spiritual gifts as a part of the whole.

The believing fellowship must be a living demonstration of the love that God gives us for one another. Our invitation to others then becomes, "Come join us in this fellowship which we have with each other and with God" (see 1 John 1:3). Before we can invite others to join our fellowship, we must *have* a fellowship. So before we can do the work of the church, we must be the church.

To do the work of reconciliation, then, we must begin by being a reconciled fellowship, by being the Body of Christ. We must model the kind of relationships into which we want to invite others. Our love for each other gives credibility and power to our witness. We must begin by *being*.

Being, though, is not complete until it results in doing. As James says, "Faith, if it has no works, is dead" (2:17). A faith that doesn't express itself in works is not a true faith. We often get volunteers who come to VOC with the goal of being reconciled to Christians of another race. Now that's good, but it's not enough. It's not enough to just be a reconciled fellowship, though that is where we have to start. We must be a reconciled fellowship *on mission*. And our mission is to bring others into fellowship with God and with us. "What we have seen and heard we proclaim to you also, that you may have fellowship with us; and indeed our fellowship is with the Father, and with His Son Jesus Christ" (1 John 1:3). John continues, "We must write and tell you about it, because the more that fellowship extends, the greater the joy it brings to us who are already in it (1 John 1:4, *Phillips*). Many of the people in the Christian community movement seem to lack this vision. They love each other, yet they lack this drive to take the gospel to unbelievers, inviting them to join the fellowship. Some of these communities reach out into their neighborhoods with social action programs, and that is great. That's part of the gospel; but it's not the whole gospel. The whole gospel speaks to both man's social needs *and* his spiritual needs.

Fellowship is not complete until the fellowship is engaged in mission. Being is not complete until it issues in doing.

If some communities make the mistake of trying to *be* without *doing*, other groups make the mistake of putting doing ahead of being. This is my tendency. When I see poverty I remember my own background and feel like "these people don't need to suffer anymore." So in my eagerness to help I sometimes put my doing ahead of my being. And if you aren't careful, I may manipulate you into putting your doing ahead of your being.

As Dolphus and I discussed the tensions that arose between us when I cut Mendenhall off from our financial support he said that I had this problem. He said I had put the ministry ahead of the people, that I had a the-program-must-go-on attitude. While Dolphus and Artis and I had 17 years together, our relationships never became very deep. They were mostly "father knows best" relationships. I was programming their lives to be what I thought they needed to be.

I'm still trying to learn to not let my doing run out ahead of my being, to not put my "ministry" ahead of people. It's not easy to learn to strike the balance between being and doing. On the one hand we must avoid just "being a fellowship," without ever getting on with the task of reaching out to others with a holistic gospel and bringing people to a saving knowledge of Jesus. On the other hand we dare not so emphasize doing that we forget that people are more important than programs. If our "ministries" ever become more important to us than people, we have forgotten what ministry is. We must learn to strike a balance.

We begin, then, by being reconciled to each other. Blacks and whites are equally damaged, equally in need of healing. Blacks come to the community with their blame and their feelings of inferiority. Whites come with their guilt and their sense of superiority. Even when these attitudes are not conscious, even when there is a real love for those of other races, with rare exceptions these attitudes are still there. Sometimes blacks or whites coming together will say, "Oh, let's don't talk about race. We don't need to talk about it." But talking about it is just exactly what we *do* need to do. Only when we've talked about it openly can healing really begin to happen.

In coming together we must expect conflict and struggle. And we have to understand each other's gimmicks. The black gimmick is to blame, to create guilt in the white. And the white likes to accept the black's problems as being his fault. The problem with that is that it removes the black person's responsibility to change the situation and encourages a patronizing response from the white person. That kind of response won't work; we must *share* the responsibility for building a better tomorrow.

I get so tired of all the cop-outs I hear at VOC. A black girl comes up with all this cheap hate against a white co-worker to get out of being efficient and committed. Or some white guy says to me, "I can't be all I want to be, because if I do I'll overshadow this black guy."

I come back, "Don't give me that patronizing garbage! Be the best you can be! If he can't perform at your level it's only because he grew up in a society that held him down and psychologically damaged him, while you grew up in a society that affirmed your whiteness. So give me the best you've got. That's what it's going to take for you to help anyone."

Community brings out the best in us. And the worst.

> Community life brings a painful revelation of our limitations, weaknesses and darkness; the unexpected discovery of the monsters within us is hard to accept. The immediate reaction is to try to destroy the monsters, or to hide them away again, pretending that they don't exist, or to flee from community life and relationships with others, or to find that the monsters are theirs, not ours. But if we accept that the monsters are there, we can let them out and learn to tame them. That is growth towards liberation.[11]

If the church is to be a racially reconciled community, it must be a fellowship where we are so secure in each other's love that we can share our feelings honestly without needing to fear rejection. We must create an environment where we can confess our sins to each other, ask each other for forgiveness, and administer God's forgiveness to each other as His priests. And we must be able to lovingly confront one another and be willing to be confronted with our own sins.

To develop a community of mutual trust, respect, and equality is not easy. It requires all the members of the community to be deeply committed to one another. And for that reconciliation to be complete, it requires a commitment to our common mission.

Reconciliation, you see, is not a warm feeling; it is love, and love always acts. Reconciliation is a unity of heart, mind, and purpose. Our reconciliation is revealed and completed as we work hand in hand to reach out to bring others into fellowship with God and with us. If we sit around and talk until we see eye to eye on everything before we do anything, we'll never do anything. But the very act of working together toward our common mission encourages the process of reconciliation.

When a community such as this is just getting started, it is a good idea for its leaders to receive guidance from the elders of another church for a while. A new group being sent out by a parent church should remain a part of that parent body until two or three of its elders have gained sufficient leadership experience to guide the community. If zealous young people take over the leadership too soon, the community members may destroy one another (see 1 Tim. 3:1-6).

Don't choose an elder who likes to lord it over others. An elder should derive his authority from his spirituality and his servant spirit.

For the ministry team about to relocate, the goal of racial reconciliation might help to determine the target area. A neighborhood changing from white to black, Spanish, or Oriental, provides an excellent opportunity for reconciliation. The fact that whites are moving out shows the need for it. The Jackson VOC is in this kind of neighborhood. If VOC had not come in, our neighborhood would probably be all black by now. As it is, the white population has stabilized at about 25 percent.

The presence or absence of a Bible-teaching church with a community outreach may also affect your choice of a target area. Do you plan to work through an existing church? Then find a church led by indigenous leaders who live in the community they serve and who share at least some of your vision for the community's renewal. If that kind of church is ministering in your target area, join it. Don't duplicate their ministry. Don't compete with it. Join forces with it. Submitting yourself to indigenous leadership will give you quicker and wider acceptance in the community.

Churches such as this, though, are rare. Obviously, if our churches in our neediest neighborhoods were effectively responding to the needs, the neighborhoods would be improving. It is precisely because the churches there are not meeting these needs that people like you need to relocate.

While the ideal situation is to be able to submit your ministry to indigenous leadership, not finding the "ideal" is no excuse for not going. Our mandate is to take the gospel. If we sit around waiting for the ideal missionary opportunity, we will never go.

What can the church you are in right now do to encourage reconciliation? One of the best possible responses is to send out a ministry team from your church to relocate into a needy area and start a new church there. The daughter church could have a rally one Sunday afternoon a month which the people from your church could pack out. You would put your offerings into the collection plate then so they could use it for their ministry with no strings attached. You could combine the rally with a potluck dinner where you could get to know the people in the new church and build bridges between blacks and whites or people of other races.

Another approach would be for your church to adopt an existing ethnic church. Have the pastor speak in your church at least once a year. Designate the offering from that service to go to the adopted church. Hold work days where people from your church help with projects at the adopted church. Combine the resources of your church with those of the adopted church to meet community needs neither church could meet alone.

Once your church has established a strong relationship with the adopted church, ask their people to join you in reaching out to other needy people in the community. For example, you could join forces to help clean up a church building or homes damaged by a storm. When you invite the people of your adopted congregation to become your partners in reaching out, they become your equals.

You personally can do things to bring about reconciliation even if you can't move into the ghetto. Turn your home and your yard into a laboratory of reconciliation by inviting people of other races to come over for a cookout together. Invite kids from the ghetto to your house. One white lady I know enrolled in a black college not only because she needed the classes but also to build relationships with blacks. She now is bringing her black friends and white friends together when she entertains in her home.

However we do it we must find ways to affirm people's dignity and help them to become all God has in mind for them to be.

You can be God's agent to bring together people now divided by sin-built walls. You can participate in God's plan in bringing healing and wholeness to our land.

You can be a reconciler!

REFLECTION

1. Can you illustrate from your own life the problem of trying to *be* without *doing* at the personal level? What about the problem of putting *being* ahead of *doing*? Which of these two tendencies do you more have to guard against?
2. What is the correct relationship between being and doing for the church fellowship? What is the church called to be? What is it called to do? How might a fellowship underemphasize doing? How might a fellowship overemphasize doing?

THE STRATEGY

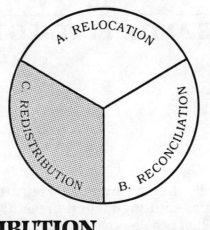

REDISTRIBUTION

15

A DIME AND A BUFFALO NICKEL

Poverty wreaks havoc throughout our world every day—
·damaging brains, stunting bodies, breaking spirits. Starvation stalks a billion people—one person out of every four alive.
Why? Because of a worldwide food shortage? No, we have
plenty of food. The problem is unequal distribution.

Claude Noel of Haiti tells this story:

Recently I was walking through the streets of a
city in Europe, contemplating the beautiful multi-
story buildings and the comfortable homes spread
all over. I turned to my wife and said, "I can more or
less understand what my father meant when in his
moments of despair he used to say, 'God is a good
provider but a poor divider.' "

My father was a hard working man and very
resourceful. But we lived on the edge of starvation.
He had come to realize, like many other people in my
land, that it is not hard work that determines
whether or not a man will feed his family. Most of the
time he fights in vain against ferocious natural elements responsible for his misery. He cannot talk

aloud about the human and social elements, so he blames it on God. My father couldn't understand why some unworthy men have more than they need while some quite worthy workers barely survive. In middle age I am just coming to discover my father's saying should be turned around: "God provides and leaves it for men to share with each other, but they do not care to do so."[12]

I was about 11 years old when I got a powerful lesson in economics which helped me see why poor families like mine stayed poor while the rich got richer.

I stood on the farmer's back porch waiting for him to come back with the money. I was bone tired, that good kind of tired that comes after a hard day's work; the kind of tired that a boy earns from doing a man's worth of hay hauling on a hot, humid summer day in Mississippi.

But if my body was remembering the day's work, my mind was flying ahead to what I could do with the dollar or dollar-and-a-half that would soon be in my pocket. Would I buy a shiny new pocket knife? That would really wow the guys back home. Or what about a wallet?

Not that I really needed these things, you see. But I was a few miles away from home. For kids in our town that was big stuff. Vacations were always an occasion for bragging. So much so that the kids who did not go on vacations had to invent them. So that's how this thing got started, this custom of buying something while you're gone to prove where you've been. So, what we bought wasn't all that important. What was important was what it would prove.

The farmer came through the kitchen onto the back porch. I held out my hand expectantly. Into it fell—I could hardly believe it—just two coins! A dime and a buffalo nickel! I stared into my hand. If that farmer would have knocked the wind out of me I couldn't have been any more surprised. Or hurt. Or humiliated.

I had been used. And there was not one thing I could do about it. Everything in me wanted to throw that blasted money on the floor and stomp out of there.

But I couldn't. I knew what white people said about "smart niggers." I knew better than to be one of those.

I shuffled off of that back porch, head down—ashamed, degraded, violated. I didn't want anyone to know. I had been exploited. I hated myself.

One question dominated my turbulent mind: "Why? Why was that farmer able to use me like that? Why did I just have to take it?" Before long, I had the answer. The farmer had the mules, the wagon, the hay, and the field. All I had was my labor and my wants. Obviously, the person with the means of production set the rules.

I was not only the farmer's victim; I was also a victim of my own values. I had let the people around me define my worth in terms of what I could buy.

I made it my goal right then to one day have my own wagon, my own mules, my own hay, and my own field, so to speak. If I didn't want to forever be exploited I would have to own my own means of production and take control of my own values. I never forgot that lesson.

My good capitalistic friends argue that American free enterprise is the best economic system ever devised. I answer, "Yes, you're right if you mean our ability to produce. That's why I support the free enterprise system. But so far we lack the *moral will* to distribute the fruits of our production in a more equitable way." Stanley Mooneyham describes the problem:

> Growth, it is now seen, is not enough in itself. Economic indicators are not accurate measuring devices where the well-being of people is concerned. Because there are strong forces which work against the poorest in even the most fair-minded societies, a rising gross national product does not mean a more equitable distribution of wealth.[13]

So production is not our problem. Our problem is unjust distribution.

Even in the U.S., in the midst of unprecedented affluence, people's basic needs—food, health care, heat, housing—go unmet. Obviously, our problem is not lack of resources; it is unequal distribution.

About six percent of the American population owns and controls 70 percent of the means of production. On the other end of the scale are 33 million Americans, 15 out of every hundred, who live below the poverty level.

In 1978 the median family income for white Americans was $18,368. For black Americans it was $10,879. The mean income per white family member was $6,422. For each black family member it was $3,588. In 1979, 8.7 percent of American whites age 14 years and over were below the poverty level. Among the same age group of blacks, 30.6 percent were below poverty. Blacks own only two percent of the nation's assets, though we comprise more than 10 percent of the population.

I don't think we have begun to comprehend the devastating effect this maldistribution is having on our country. Our society promotes the abortion of black babies because it is unwilling to pay the price of redistribution. Although opposition to abortion is almost unanimous among poor American blacks, 30 percent of the abortions performed in abortion clinics are on blacks. According to Dr. Charles Greenlee, a respected black physician in Pittsburgh, public assistance workers coerce indigent black women into visiting abortion clinics. They implicitly and explicitly threaten to cut off welfare payments if the mother has more children.[14]

I believe that these young women are victims of the rich. Blacks don't want abortion. But when a black teenage girl is confronted by an intimidating, well-educated white social worker who advocates abortion, what chance does she have?

It appears to the blacks that the rich are promoting abortion as an alternative to redistribution. Unwilling to redistribute, to share with the poor, it seems that the rich seek to destroy them, that they try to eliminate poverty through "population control," physically eliminating the poor.

The unjust distribution of resources is also filling our prisons and mental hospitals with blacks. The rich, through advertising, create a craving for affluence among the poor. They feed them the lie that money can buy happiness. Then this same society which exhorts the poor to climb out of poverty withholds the means to do it. The poor ask for skills and jobs; society gives them dehumanizing welfare programs that stifle their motivation, rob them of their dignity. The "carrot" of the "good life" remains forever beyond their reach. The resulting frustration may lead to violence and mental illness. It is no coincidence that 70 percent of our prison inmates are black and that mental illness is not uncommon among blacks. In a society that systematically cultivates greed then denies its people the means to satisfy that greed, such an end is inevitable.

The poor are now beginning to realize that the greed and luxury of others is causing their suffering. Desperate millions, with nothing left to lose, are resorting to violence. They are becoming wise to the rich who are trying to manipulate them into fighting their economic wars for them. They will no longer believe the rhetoric of fear which labels every effort of the poor to help themselves as "Communist" or 'Socialist."

At the height of the civil rights movement in the sixties I was listening to Senator James O. Eastland of Mississippi on the radio. I knew that the senator owned 5,000 acres of the Mississippi Delta. I had heard that at one time he was getting $250,000 of government subsidy for not planting crops on his land. And I knew that he was voting against every human rights bill for the poor that came along—including those designed to help the starving children on his own plantation.

Senator Eastland was reporting on his recent trip to South Africa where a tiny minority of whites dominates a nation of blacks, depriving them of their human rights. The senator said, "I stood on the borders of South Africa and watched those Communist insurgents come in and attack the people of South Africa."

When I heard him say that I felt like joining those rebels. All these brave young men wanted was the right to self-determination in their own land. And he was calling them Communist infiltrators.

That kind of simplistic labeling simply won't stand up in the days ahead. The poor will not be written off that easily. We are going to have to grapple with how to redistribute God's resources more justly in our society.

Those South African rebels wanted nothing more than what the American poor want—the right of self-determination. Unless we make major changes in our response to the poor which give them a genuine basis for hope, I believe we must expect a renewed wave of violence in the American ghettos. James Tillman observes:

Unless the middle-class and other non-poor

THE PYRAMID OF AMERICAN SOCIETY

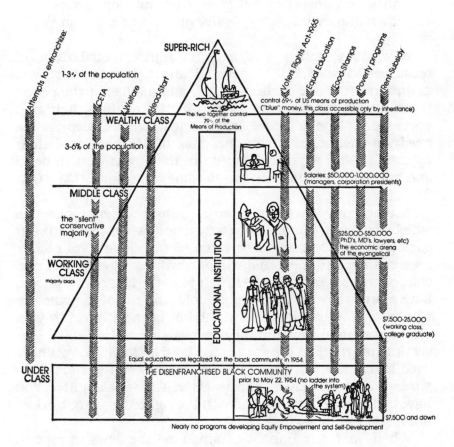

Attempts to enfranchize:

CETA

Welfare

Head-Start

SUPER-RICH

1-3% of the population

The two together control
79% of the
Means of Production

control 69% of US means of production
("blue" money, this class accessible only by inheritance)

Voters Rights Act 1965

Equal Education

Food-Stamps

Poverty programs

Rent-Subsidy

WEALTHY CLASS

3-6% of the population

Salaries: $50,000-1,000,000
(managers, corporation presidents)

MIDDLE CLASS

the "silent"
conservative
majority

$25,000-$50,000
(PhD's, MD's, lawyers, etc)
the economic arena
of the evangelical

WORKING
CLASS
majority black

EDUCATIONAL INSTITUTION

$7,500-25,000
(working class,
college graduate)

Equal education was legalized for the black community in 1954.

UNDER
CLASS

THE DISENFRANCHISED BLACK COMMUNITY
prior to May 22, 1954 (no ladder into
the system)

$7,500 and down

Nearly no programs developing Equity Empowerment and Self-Development undertake radical and revolutionary changes in both their thinking and behavior towards the poor, this period today must be viewed as the period in which the middle-class succeeded in convincing the poor that the middle-class *is* the enemy. It must also be viewed as the period in which, because of the negative use of naked power by the middle-class, the poor succeeded in ridding themselves of the guilt which hitherto had prevented them from moving against the non-poor through *effective group confrontation.*[15]

How does God speak to our unjust distribution of resources? Psalm 140:12 says, "I know that the Lord will maintain the cause of the afflicted, and justice for the poor." God's justice for the poor is also justice against their rich oppressors: "Woe to those," Isaiah cried, "who . . . deprive the needy of justice, and rob the poor of My people of their rights. . . . Now what will you do in the day of punishment, and in the devastation which will come from afar?" (Isa. 10:1-3).

"Come now, you rich, weep and howl for your miseries which are coming upon you. Your riches have rotted and your garments have become moth-eaten. Your gold and your silver have rusted; and their rust will be a witness against you and will consume your flesh like fire. It is in the last days that you have stored up your treasure! Behold, the pay of the laborers who mowed your fields, and which has been withheld by you, cries out against you; and the outcry of those who did the harvesting has reached the ears of the Lord of Sabaoth. You have lived luxuriously on the earth and led a life of wanton pleasure; you have fattened your hearts in a day of slaughter. You have condemned and put to death the righteous man; he does not resist you" (Jas. 5:1-6).

When John the Baptist commanded the Jews to repent, the people asked, "Then what shall we do?"

John answered, "Let the man who has two tunics share with him who has none; and let him who has food do likewise" (Luke 3:10,11).

Paul wrote to the Corinthians, ". . . at this present time your abundance being a supply for their want, that their abundance also may become a supply for your want, that there may be equality" (2 Cor. 8:14).

When God was ready to bring His chosen people into the Promised Land, He established laws to ensure just distribution of resources. First, He commanded that the land be divided equally among the people. Then He decreed that if anyone became so poor that he had to sell his land, a kinsman would have the first right to buy it—to "redeem" it and keep it within the family. Still, God knew that over the years of buying and selling, people would selfishly accumulate land for themselves at the expense of the poor. Equality would be lost.

So God instituted jubilee. "On the day of atonement you shall sound a horn all through your land. You shall thus consecrate the fiftieth year and proclaim a release through the land to all its inhabitants. It shall be a jubilee for you, and each of you shall return to his own property, and each of you shall return to his family" (Lev. 25:9,10). The land could not be sold permanently. Why? Because the people did not own it. God owned it. The people were only aliens and sojourners— God's guests and stewards of God's resources (see Lev. 25:23).

That truth—that we are not owners, but stewards— demands today, as then, an equitable distribution of the world's resources. We who are rich have no inherent "right" to lavish on ourselves all the comforts and conveniences we can afford. The earth and its resources do not belong to us at all, but to God. God did not provide His bounty for the few, but for all. Therefore, those who have more than enough are responsible before God to share with those who have less than enough.

We know that God demands justice and equality. Yet we need only to look around to see that our resources are not distributed fairly. God's justice demands that we redistribute our resources.

The typical response to God's demand for redistribution is that of the rich young ruler: "He went away grieved; for he was one who owned much property" (Matt. 19:22). Many of us fail to understand what Jesus was asking the young man.

When Jesus asked the rich young man to sell his goods and give to the poor, he did not say, "Become destitute and friendless." Rather he said, "Come, fol-

low me" (Matt. 19:21). In other words, he invited him
to join a community of sharing and love, where his
security would not be based on individual property
holdings, but on openness to the Spirit and on the
loving care of new-found brothers and sisters.[16]

We resist giving up our possessions because we fail to see
that that which we hold fast is the very thing that separates
us from the abundant life God has in store for us.

As a first step toward redistribution, then, we must commit ourselves to living with less in order that we can share
more. This process of finding ways to use less can be a lifelong
family adventure. Yet living more simply will not in itself make
much difference in the lives of the poor. We must find ways to
use what we save to empower the needy.

Now, usually when I mention redistribution, people think
I'm talking about taking all the money from the rich and giving it to the poor. That wouldn't help a bit! If today you took all
the money from the rich and gave it to the poor, the rich
would have it back within a few days. Why? Because the poor
would go out and spend all their money on Cadillacs, fur
coats, suede shoes and whiskey—empty symbols of
"success"—rather than on the means of production.

The kind of redistribution we need must go far beyond a
dependency-creating welfare system. It must go far beyond
the church's little 10 percent charity, very little of which ever
gets to the poor anyway. Our redistribution must involve us—
our time, our energy, our gifts, and our skills. If we are sharing ourselves, sharing our money will follow naturally.

H. Spees used to meet with a group of Jackson businessmen for a prayer breakfast and Bible study. He began to talk to
them about how authentic faith shows concern for the disenfranchised. Some of these men were really moved by that. One
of the men came to H. and said, "You know, H., in the circles I
move in I don't see any poor people. But I want to help. I want
to create a fund with Voice of Calvary Ministries to help people
who are genuinely poor. Whenever this fund is depleted, you
let me know and I'll add some more money to it."

H. came back from this meeting just beaming and told me
what had just happened. And I told him, "Look, go back to

this businessman and tell him that the poor need more than just his money. The poor need his skills, his business mind, his ability to organize things. We need *him*, not just his money."

It wasn't long before this brother was involved in our ministry. A Christmas or so ago he was walking with us up and down the streets, visiting and helping the poor. When we dedicated our Thriftco co-op in Edwards, he spoke, sharing his concern and vision for the poor. Now his whole family shares his concern for the poor and oppressed in our society.

The poor need something more than handouts. They need the means to build a better life for themselves. We must bring into the poor community the basic education the people need. We must motivate them. We must teach them the vocational and management skills required to start community-based economic enterprises. When necessary, we must support these enterprises with skills of Christian professionals from outside the community—accountants, computer technicians, architects, engineers, attorneys, and so on. And we must come up with creative strategies to generate starting capital for these enterprises. (Chapter 18 suggests several options.) To achieve real redistribution, real economic justice, we must redistribute the means of production.

God commands economic justice. The tottering economy, the widening gap between rich and poor, and the resultant tensions of crime, hostility, and war all remind us of how massively God's command is being disobeyed. In contrast, God promised prosperity, peace, and protection if His people would obey His plan of economic justice prescribed in the jubilee. He declared:

"If you walk in My statutes and keep My commandments so as to carry them out, then I shall give you your rains in their season, so that the land will yield its produce. . . . You will thus eat your food to the full and live securely in your land. I shall also grant peace in the land, so that you may lie down with no one making you tremble . . . and no sword will pass through your land. . . . I will also walk among you and be your God, and you shall be My people" (Lev. 26:3-6, 12).

According to God's Word, no amount of military might, no arsenal of nuclear warheads will bring peace or security to our nation. Our nation will have true peace and prosperity when and only when it obeys God.

Let us demonstrate justice throughout our land that the world may know that He is our God and we are His people.

REFLECTION

1. What social problems in America result at least partially from the maldistribution of our economic resources? How does maldistribution effect the rate of abortion among blacks? The high black prison population?
2. How does the Bible speak to the unjust distribution of resources? What is jubilee? What truth is it based on?
3. By redistribution, the author does not mean taking money from the rich and giving it to the poor. What does he mean?
4. According to Scripture, what is the only true basis for peace and national security? Why does the author believe that a more just distribution of our nation's economic resources would contribute to peace and national security? Do you agree? Why or why not?
5. What do you think most Americans look to as the basis for peace and national security? If you did not answer "obedience to God," what do you think may be some of the consequences of this misplaced trust?

16

THE NOT-SO-GREAT SOCIETY

I was speaking at a week-long missions conference at a church in Philadelphia. As the days passed, my fancy hotel room started to feel a bit stuffy. I began to want to get out with some of our people. So one day I asked one of the young brothers who had been coming to the meetings to show me where our people lived.

The next morning he picked me up at my room and drove me to the neighborhood where he had grown up. We drove through the streets until finally glass and debris kept us from going any farther. We parked the car and started walking. As we came up to this dilapidated apartment building, so run-down that I assumed it was abandoned, my friend saw someone he knew—his cousin. "Let's go in and visit," he said.

Two guys and two gals were smoking dope in a room pulsing with blaring music and flashing lights. One of the guys spent the first few minutes trying to convince me that smoking dope was better than drinking whiskey. He was calling one of the girls there his "lady." "What do you mean, 'your lady'?" I asked.

"That means we're not married but we have a family together."

"How many children do you have with your lady?"

"I have three and she has two," he answered.

I kept probing. "Why aren't you married to her?"

"It's a better arrangement for us not to be married so she can get welfare and food stamps and I can still be here."

"Do you work?"

"Yeah, I work as a guard but I get paid in cash, so my wages aren't reported to the government. That way I can get food stamps too."

Then I noticed another girl, about 21 years old, getting ready to leave with her four or five kids behind her. "Who is she?" I asked.

"She's my lady's sister," he told me.

"How many children does she have?"

"She has five kids too. She's not married either, but she has her man." He must have sensed my surprise because he added, "Well, their younger sister is 18 and she's got four kids."

These young folks were trapped in a welfare system where the easiest way to get more money was to have more kids. So naturally, that's what they did. The welfare system encouraged them to have more kids, to live together without getting married, and to lie to qualify for food stamps. It gave them no incentive at all to get out of their situation.

A few months ago in Nashville a young man was showing me an apartment complex run by the housing authority. About 4,000 people lived there. We walked up to a group of teenage girls and guys sitting on their cars blowing dope. My host introduced me as a Christian cooperative organizer and author and said I was going to be speaking on community development that evening in the community center. The kids sounded interested. One girl, about 16 years old, said, "I really want to come because I really want me a job."

Quite a few of the kids came that evening. The 16-year-old girl came in late. At the end of the meeting, she kept saying with deep emotion, "Mister, I need a job. I need a skill so I can get me a job. I want to be able to take care of my own child. I want to be able to raise my child like a real woman."

After the meeting I asked one of the guys, "Does she have a child?"

"No," he answered. "She doesn't have a husband either. During the four years I've been working at the community center here in this apartment complex, I have only known of three or four families where a husband and wife have lived in an apartment together for any length of time. The housing authority program is set up so that if a family makes more than $8,000 they can't live here. So usually we end up with households headed by women without husbands."

Because of the environment this housing authority program had created, this teenage girl had no dream of getting married and raising a family. Her highest ambition was to be a self-sufficient single parent. That was the only model of strong womanhood she had.

People are living out thousands of stories like this all across our nation this very moment. Well-intentioned government programs designed to relieve the poor actually turn the poor into dependent cripples. They treat symptoms without touching causes. The poor, then, become addicted to the temporary relief offered by the welfare programs, and temporary relief stretches into permanent dependence. The incentive to solve the underlying social and economic problems is destroyed by the programs which provide relief from symptoms.

Even Senator Edward Kennedy has conceded that our present programs are ineffective. Our greatest problem, according to Kennedy, is the breakup of the home, and there is no social welfare program that can deal with that. It is a moral problem.

One of the greatest enemies of the American black family today is the welfare system. Designed to assist when there was no father, the welfare system stepped in and replaced the father. It eliminated the need for families to take economic initiative. It rewarded mothers if the husbands did not come back, and penalized them if they did.

I know of young mothers in Mississippi who moved to New York, Michigan, or California for one reason—to get on welfare. In the sixties the highest-paid domestic worker in Mendenhall made four dollars a day—far less than she could have gotten on welfare in some Northern cities.

I know of families who could be earning extra income by

renting out an extra bedroom, but they don't do it because it would affect their eligibility for food stamps. The welfare system all too often makes it unprofitable to work. It penalizes two-parent families. It destroys initiative and drive. Our nation's welfare system is destroying the black family.

While we must provide temporary relief to the needy, we must not make relief the permanent response. We must treat the cause of the problem and eliminate the need for relief.

> There are two kinds of service—social service and social action. Social service treats symptoms, social action treats causes. Social service is the Band-Aid; social action is the surgery. Social service takes a food basket to a needy family at Christmas; social action tries to eliminate the conditions which produce the hunger. Social service visits a man in prison; social action reforms a penal system so primitive and barbarous its primary tool for correcting behavior is still punishment. Social service sends the Red Cross to Vietnam; social action uses every means at its disposal to end the Vietnam War.[17]

Our government poverty programs fall short because their designers have failed to distinguish between strategies that treat only symptoms and thus lead to dependency, and those that result in development, breaking the cycle of poverty and eliminating the need for continued relief. U.S. poverty programs, therefore, have been a mixture of good and bad, effective and ineffective, constructive and destructive.

Let's look at housing. On the positive side, the Farmer's Home Administration home mortgage program and the Federal Housing Administration, both known as FHA, are two of the best government programs for low- and middle-income families because they encourage *home ownership*. That is important for two reasons. First, home ownership strengthens the family. So many of our government programs make the children their starting point. One result is that the responsibility for the child's welfare seems to shift from the parents to the service agency. And this shift often weakens the family structure, as we have seen.

A better approach is to focus on the whole family

structure—not just the kids. One way to do this is through programs which encourage home ownership. Owning a home pulls a family together and encourages the parents to take responsibility for their children.

Home ownership is also valuable precisely because it is *ownership*. The poor own very little. They often spend almost everything on consumer goods and almost nothing on savings or investments. As long as that pattern continues, they will stay poor.

In contrast to the Farmers' Home Administration mortgage program, the housing authority program of HUD has not been very effective in helping the poor. This program has put most of its money into subsidized high-rise apartments that have become rat-infested crime dens. The problem is that the landlords are the ones being subsidized. The people living there never get any ownership.

Once I was talking with some of the staff members of the housing authority in Atlanta. They asked me, "What can we do to help change the dehumanizing conditions of these apartment buildings?"

My answer was simple, "Give the apartments to the people."

They thought I was crazy. But that's exactly what we need to do. These apartments can be turned into cooperatives or condominiums. Rent subsidies need to be replaced with mortgage-payment subsidies. We don't need a new program or any more money to do this at all. We just need to redirect the subsidies to the poor family and subsidize home ownership among the poor, rather than to subsidize landlords and local and county government housing authorities.

Ownership creates responsibility. If I go into one of these housing authority apartments and see a broken screen and ask, "Why isn't your screen fixed?" the mother may answer, "The landlord hasn't gotten around to fixing it yet."

Then if I ask, "Who broke it?" she'll say, "My kids broke it." Her lack of ownership has removed her sense of responsibility. If she owned the apartment, she would feel responsible enough to fix it herself. She would also feel responsible to teach her children to take care of the apartment.

The key to redistribution and empowerment of the poor is

helping people to accept responsibility for their own development.

If HUD would quit subsidizing landlords, and give that subsidy to people buying their own homes, they could phase each family off of the subsidy as they built up equity. Say, for example, that once a family had $12,000 equity in a home they could no longer qualify for a mortgage subsidy—or, for that matter, for food stamps or welfare. Forced to choose between keeping the house and staying on the subsidy program, most families would choose to keep the house. The poor family would be on its way to self-sufficiency, the taxpayers would save money, and the housing industry would be stimulated because of the increased demand for housing. Since all the materials used to build houses can be produced right here in our own nation, our whole national economy would benefit.

Government also has a mixed record in the area of employment programs. The CETA program (Comprehensive Employment and Training Act) was designed to develop employable skills through on-the-job training—a good idea. However, the program seldom achieved its goal. VOC used to use CETA workers. But these young people weren't working for us; they were working for city hall. They were just assigned to us. So it was hard for us to hold them accountable for their work.

Many of the CETA jobs were almost meaningless. They gave the young people income with little responsibility. Some of our best kids would get these jobs. Then if I offered them a really productive job where they could get $3.00 an hour while learning a useful skill, they would say, "Why should I work for you for $3.00 an hour when I can get more working for CETA?"

What we need are programs that teach marketable skills, not programs that just offer temporary unskilled employment. We need job programs that lead to employment.

Work incentive programs need to be operated through the people who own the businesses. To begin with, only businesses which have the capacity to keep the newly-trained workers on the payroll should qualify for the program. Not only should the trainee be subsidized, but the employer should receive a little subsidy for the expense of training the new worker. In return, the employer would make a commitment to provide a regular job to the young man or woman once he or she satisfactorily completed the training. If the employer failed to keep his commitment to hire the person, he would be required to return a portion of his training expense subsidy. This kind of program would lead to development, not dependence.

One of the best, most compassionate programs ever created by the government is the Head Start program. Dr. Robert Cole and others did a study of the effects of poverty on the development and education of children in Mississippi. They convinced President Kennedy and later President Johnson of the need for an early childhood education program that would give these kids a head start. In addition to education, the Head Start program provided the children with nutritious meals, dental care, and medical checkups, which they would not have gotten otherwise.

Its weakness was that there was no easy way to build a sense of permanence, a sense of community ownership into it. The program provided money to rent buildings and equipment, but provided little money for ownership. The program wasn't set up to encourage the community, the Head Start families, to go together and create a permanent Head Start center which they would own. In spite of this, a few communities found ways to provide permanent Head Start facilities for their children, and these have proven to be highly valuable to the program.

Besides the lack of community ownership we found another serious problem with the program. In Mississippi the program was initially open only to families with incomes below $3,500. In 1966 a large plant in our area which had not previously employed blacks except as janitors started to hire blacks. All of a sudden, some families were making $6,000. They no longer qualified for Head Start. The children from those families had to drop out of the program, even though they still needed it as much as before. We now have our own program, Genesis One, which is open to students in our community that do not qualify for Head Start.

One nutrition program that has been effective is WIC—Women, Infants, and Children. By providing nutritious food to pregnant and nursing mothers it prevents mental retardation and other health problems that would otherwise not only bring much suffering, but would also impose a heavy financial burden on society.

The health initiative program which provided the start-up money for two of our four health centers is an example of a valuable government program. Although it has had its problems, the program has helped bring health care into neglected rural communities where there has been little or no health service for many years.

The health initiative program was created through the leadership of blacks and a few concerned whites. The old white establishment which controlled the existing health care delivery system opposed the program, seeing any new service as a threat to them.

Even many poor whites in Mississippi opposed the health initiative program, even though they needed it as much as poor blacks. Why? Because the whites who controlled the Mississippi economy fanned the flame of racial hatred. If a program would help blacks, that alone was promoted as reason enough to oppose it. The poor white, who often has little sense of self-worth, finds a sort of perverse affirmation of his worth through his hatred. His hatred makes him feel superior to those he hates.

We need to show the poor white that the poor black is not his enemy; his enemy is a racist economic system based on greed and self-interest which exploits poor black and poor white alike. We need to show the black poor and the white poor that we face a common enemy. The poor must quit fighting each other and turn their energies to the common task of development—of creating a society with economic justice.

In general, those government programs which have provided medical care, nutrition, education, job skills, and ownership have proven effective weapons against poverty. Other programs have all too often created dependency, robbed their clients of a sense of responsibility, and turned their so-called beneficiaries into victims.

Our federal government, no doubt, has a serious responsibility to the poor. But given its poor record of ineffectiveness, it is foolish to expect our government to lead the way in providing creative, constructive and nurturing social services.

We Christians must assume far more responsibility for shaping compassionate, effective, community-based responses to the poor. We must provide the leadership. We must become personally involved in providing services to the poor in ways that affirm their dignity and reflect God's love and concern for them.

Then we must work with government leaders to help them understand how government can support these community-based programs with funding and technicians. We can form a new, creative partnership with our government leaders which acknowledges that we need their help and interaction and that they need our help and interaction. In this new partnership, though, the government will not be sending outsiders to impose Washington's solutions on the needy; rather, the federal government will be supporting and encouraging community-based programs which have been designed and are being led by people in the community of need—people who know the people's needs firsthand.

The government cutback of social programs offers the church a golden opportunity as never before. For far too long we have neglected our scriptural responsibility to the poor with the excuse that "that's the government's job." We should never expect the government to provide for the needs of the poor without the Christian's active involvement. The only institution in America with the human resources adequate to meet the needs of the poor is the church. But racism and misguided patriotism have blinded the church to this great mission opportunity. Only the church carries the Good News of Jesus Christ which, when lived out faithfully, responds to the total needs of the poor—physical, social, and spiritual—in ways that affirm the dignity and self worth of the individual.

The cutback in government social programs also offers us a fresh opportunity for real patriotism. I am convinced that you and I, as American citizens, can do nothing more patriotic than to take the gospel to the poor in a way that meets their deep-felt needs, brings them into a personal relationship with Jesus Christ, and then includes them in a local Body which sees itself as Christ's visible presence in that local community.

REFLECTION

1. This chapter opens with some examples of how a well-intentioned welfare program victimizes those it was designed to help. Can you add any examples of your own?
2. The author believes that the government's role in assisting the poor with housing should be to promote home ownership—not to subsidize rent. Do you agree? Why or why not?
3. Where does the author draw the line between an effective and an ineffective jobs program?
4. What are some of the strengths and weaknesses of the Head Start program? How could the weaknesses be corrected?
5. In general, which government programs have been most effective in fighting poverty? Would you say that most government programs have been effective or ineffective?
6. The author calls for a radical change in the federal government's role in relation to the problems of our poor. What is the nature of this called-for change?
7. What role does the author believe the church should have in relation to our nation's poor? Do you agree or disagree? Why?

CAN FREE ENTERPRISE WORK FOR US?

What kind of economic system is the most Christian? To many the answer seems self-evident—free enterprise.

I would like to agree. I enjoy the opportunity free enterprise offers me. But I cannot agree fully. Along with its advantages, free enterprise is handicapped by a serious flaw—man's greed. Both biblical history and American history remind us repeatedly that greedy men will use economic freedom to exploit—to profit at the expense of others. Employers pay employees as little as possible in order to maximize their own profits rather than treating their employee's economic interests as being as important as their own—or, to be thoroughly Christian—more important than their own.

Advertisers create markets for products which no one needs, not from a motive of servanthood, but out of greed, pure and simple. Businesses measure their success primarily by their financial profits—not by how well they glorify God and serve people. What a far cry we are from a truly Christian economy!

A truly Christian economic system would begin with the fact that the earth is the Lord's, not ours, and that God and

God alone has the authority to determine how His wealth will be used. Our job as stewards is to carry out His will. A Christian economic system would recognize that God provides the earth's resources for *all* mankind, not just for some. It would be designed to distribute God's resources to all humanity in some sort of equitable way.

Free enterprise, as it now exists, falls far short of God's standard. It has failed to distribute the earth's resources equitably. And when Christianity should have been calling the American free enterprise system to account for its immoral stewardship, it was instead "baptizing" the system, adopting free enterprise as an implicit "article of faith." Free enterprise has become almost a religious doctrine that justifies our greed and substitutes token charity for real economic justice. It enables us to blame the victims of oppression for their own poverty and lets us feel little responsibility to redistribute our wealth to the needy. The result of such a system is predictable—increasing production by the rich, but continuing poverty for the oppressed.

Communism, then, came along as an attempt to distribute the earth's resources more equitably. Communism sprang into being because apostate religion could not challenge man's greed. But atheistic communism has not brought justice either.

Neither capitalism nor communism can bring justice to the poor. Once we have seen what God's Word means by economic justice, that is self-evident. While some economic systems are better than others, no system will serve the people well as long as those who control it are motivated by greed. We as Christians must champion an alternative. We must create a system that is based not on greed, not even on greed tempered by honesty (the ideal of free enterprise), but on justice and love. We must create a system that distributes wealth more equitably in response to human needs. This Christian economic system will by its very existence be a prophetic voice to the world system.

Selfish, unregenerated man will never develop this type of system. We, the people of God, must do it or it will never be done at all.

How do we begin to shape a just economy?

First, we must understand where our economy stands now. When man has abused his economic freedom, using it to produce an unjust distribution of resources, corrective action is called for. The economic plight of American blacks today has its roots in slavery and in the center of oppression which followed emancipation. It is like a baseball game. In the ninth inning the team which is trailing 20 to 2 discovers that the winning team has been cheating all along. The leading team admits, "Yes, we were cheating, but we'll play fair now. Let's go out and finish the game."

Now, it's good that the team is going to quit cheating, but with the score 20 to 2 the trailing team still has the feeling they're going to lose. When injustice has been done, establishing justice means something more than "playing fair from now on."

In America today, one group has the capital, the other has the labor and the broken spirit. We say to the trailing team, "Get onto the field and play. You are now equal. You don't need affirmative action. You don't need special access to job training. You don't need any kind of special help; that would be reverse discrimination. You are now equal and free."

Achieving justice in America will require something more than "playing fair from now on." Economic opportunity in capitalism depends on ownership of capital. The free enterprise system assumes that anyone can have access to capital through his labor and that banks and lending institutions will make investment capital available to anyone who has the will and the know-how to produce goods and services for the marketplace. There is only one problem with that assumption—it's not true.

The oppressed among us know all too well that the oppressive forces which created their poverty in the first place keep them trapped in it. The young black electrician, having never had an opportunity to establish a credit rating, finds it almost impossible to raise the capital to buy the tools and equipment to go into business for himself. The general rule is, "To get capital, you must have capital," and so the system perpetuates and widens the gap between rich and poor.

Despites its serious failures I don't want to throw out the free enterprise system. The freedom which many use to satisfy their greed can also be used to develop economic enterprises not based on greed. The free enterprise system gives us the freedom to create businesses designed to serve, rather than to exploit. If we Christians will devote our capital and ourselves to creating such a system, we can make just such a system work. And it can all be done within the context of free enterprise.

One of the best tools for making free enterprise work for the poor is the cooperative. A cooperative is a business that people operate to get goods and services they want. It is formed when people who may have little capital pool their resources to do things none of them could do individually. Those who use the cooperative own and control it. Any "profit" is returned to the co-op's members, in proportion to how much they use the co-op, through lower prices or patronage refunds. A co-op, then, exists to serve the people who use it.

Cooperatives operate according to four basic principles:

1. *Open membership.* Anyone who wants to may join a cooperative, regardless of race or creed. No one, however, is required to join to use its services.

2. *One person, one vote.* The members run the business democratically. Each member, no matter how great his investment or how large his patronage, has one vote. Members usually use their votes to choose directors who then set co-op policies.

3. *Patronage refunds.* This gets to the heart of the difference between cooperatives and other types of businesses. The purpose of a co-op is to meet people's needs for products and services as economically as possible—not to make money for investors as non-cooperative businesses must do.

At the end of the year, any "profits" are distributed to co-op members, in proportion to how much they have used the co-op, as patronage refunds.

4. *Limited return on investments.* In most co-ops, the members are the major investors. The return that can be paid to them *as investors* is limited. That is, a few members cannot make large, controlling investments and drain off the benefits from the other members. In co-ops, benefits are distributed according to patronage (use), rather than investment.

Since co-ops are new to most people, the members need to

be constantly educated in cooperative principles so they can operate their co-op effectively. If a co-op is serving its members well, they will demand increased services which will in turn force expansion. A co-op should always be ready to grow to increase its capacity to serve its members.

There are three major kinds of cooperatives.

Marketing co-ops sell and process farm products. The farmers who use the co-ops own them. Some of these co-ops have well-known brand name products, such as Sunkist, Sun Maid, Welch, and Ocean Spray.

Purchasing co-ops operate retail stores (such as food stores), service stations, or feed mills. The customers own these co-ops.

Service co-ops furnish electricity, insurance, housing, health care, credit, nursery schools, funeral services, etc. They are owned by the people who use the services.

How do you start a cooperative? The first step is simply to talk to a few others who would benefit from the kind of co-op you have in mind. Once several of you have agreed that you want to form a certain kind of co-op you are ready to call a meeting of potential co-op members.

To get ready for this meeting, select an adviser. This might be anyone who knows how to start a co-op—your county extension agent, your state cooperative council secretary, or a co-op manager. Plan your first meeting with his help. For technical help and publications, you might want to write to one of the following organizations:

- Southern Cooperative Development Fund
  P.O. Box 3885
  Lafayette, LA 70501

- Economics, Statistics, and Cooperative Service Cooperative Program
  U.S. Department of Agriculture
  Washington, D.C. 20250

- The Cooperative League
  1828 L Street Northwest
  Washington, D.C. 20036

• Federation of Southern Cooperatives
  P.O. Box 95
  Epes, Alabama 35460

At the meeting, carefully explain the proposal. Invite questions and discussion on the matter. If interest in starting the co-op is high enough to move ahead, form a committee to survey all aspects of the proposed cooperative with the adviser's help. Set a date for the second meeting when the survey team will report back.

The survey committee goes to work. It surveys potential members to see if the co-op will have enough business to make it work. It begins looking for a manager, for a place to locate the business, for possible loans. It develops an operating budget and determines how much each member would need to invest.

At the second meeting, the potential members discuss the survey committee's report in detail. It may take more than one meeting for the group to agree on a plan of action.

Once a plan is settled on, if there are enough people willing to invest the time and money to make the co-op work, the group selects an organizing committee. With the legal advice of a lawyer, this organizing committee drafts articles of incorporation, bylaws, and so on. They sign up members and deposit their money.

At the first meeting of the members, bylaws are adopted and the first board of directors is elected—if they are not named in the charter (articles of incorporation).

The board of directors meets at once to get the co-op started. It elects officers, hires a manager, and takes the other steps necessary to open the business.

What does a cooperative, a business built on these principles, look like? Let's take a look at Thriftco, VOC's cooperative retail store in Mendenhall, Jackson, and Edwards.

If you were to walk into a Thriftco store you would find a modern, clean, attractive, well-designed store. It would remind you of a discount department store such as K-Mart. You would, however, find that you could buy good merchandise for much less than you could at other stores. Much of the merchandise in the store would be new. Some of the clothing, furniture, and appliances would have been recycled at Thrift-co's recycling center.

If you bought something, the cashier would invite you to join the co-op. By buying a $5.00 share, you would become one of the owners of the store and receive a five percent discount on all purchases. As an owner you would share equally with all other shareholders in setting store policy, primarily through the co-op's annual meeting.

You would sense something different about this store. Its whole reason for existence is to serve you. It doesn't just "serve" you in order to make a profit for its owners. This goal of service is expressed in the store's statement of objectives:

● To provide essential household and clothing items to poor families at low cost.

● To develop and solidify an economic base in the poor and black rural community.

● To encourage the development of local black leadership.

● To provide a source of income to support local Christian ministries.

● To provide employment and management training in the community.

● To provide a vehicle for organizing and mobilizing poor people and getting them involved in the social, political, and economic destinies of their own community.

● To engage people, especially the poor, in ownership of their own economic enterprises.

● To provide an opportunity for churches and individuals to become involved with the poor in a constructive way through donating goods and labor.

Another form of cooperative business is a mutual savings and loan association—a savings and loan owned by its depositors. In Jackson I serve on the board of State Mutual Savings and Loan, a bank which makes loans primarily in the ghetto area.

Located in the heart of a Pittsburgh slum is Dwelling House Savings and Loan, which is powerfully demonstrating how a bank can minister to the poor. Its motto is, "the institution that serves your need, not our greed." It makes high-risk loans to mostly poor people who cannot get credit from other lending institutions.

Executive vice-president Robert R. Lavelle approaches his work as an inner-city banker totally as a Christian ministry. "It seems to me that the whole needs of man have to be met. His soul must be touched so he can be aware of relationships in something other than a dependent sense.

"Our effort is still to lend in a poor area," Bob explains. "This violates the banking rule of lending high at the lowest risk, for poor and black people are always the highest risk and the lowest return.

"When we provide home ownership opportunities (equity) to poor and black people, the economics of their areas can change from dope, numbers, prostitution, pimps, and loan sharks, to home ownership, good city services, police and garbage collection, quality schools, viable businesses, and jobs."

Bob visits customers who fall behind on their monthly mortgage payments, encouraging them not to give up, offering them lessons in household economics.

He refuses to let his bank guard carry a gun. "Money isn't worth shooting anyone over," he insists. Instead, his weapon, his sword, has been the Word of God. In fact, Bob has witnessed to many of the robbers who have held up the bank over the years.

Bob himself earns only $10,000 a year. He even gave up his salary for a couple of years to avoid laying off an employee. Christians and other friends across the country help to make this ministry to Pittsburgh's poor possible by keeping savings accounts at Dwelling House.

"What I try to do," he says, "is show my Christian commitment to be an everyday affair. Christ was in the marketplace. We keep talking about how we have to be practical. Well, not many are willing to test the practicality of Jesus' message."

But in Pittsburgh's Hill district, the gospel's practicality has been put to the test. Since Bob took over the bank in 1957, home ownership has risen from 12 percent to about 35 percent today.

By the world's standards, Robert Lavelle might not be a smashing success. He has turned down numerous offers for "bigger and better" positions and has fought off suggestions that he move to a "nicer" location where he could attract more lucrative middle-class business. "We may not grow as exponentially as the others," he says, "but we have to make up our mind what our mission is." (For more information, write: Dwelling House, 501 Herron Ave., Pittsburgh, PA 15219.)

Two other kinds of co-ops can benefit a poor community— the credit union and an investment corporation. In many communities the best co-op to start with is a credit union. One of the most important ways to help poor families to get a handle on their finances is to get them to start saving regularly. That's the biggest value of a credit union. A credit union also creates capital. It makes loans to its members at reasonable rates (usually 12 percent) for such things as furniture, appliances, cars, and home improvements.

An investment corporation is a financial cooperative with the purpose of financing business development. A long-time dream of mine, the National Christian Investment Corporation, is now being formed. This organization will make loans at affordable rates for community economic development projects throughout the country, investing in projects which promote the kingdom of Jesus Christ.

Financing is available to qualifying co-ops at reasonable rates through such institutions as the Southern Cooperative Development Fund which I helped to create, and the National Cooperative Consumer Bank in Washington, D.C.

A Christian organization which works for economic development among the third-world poor is the Institute for International Development, Incorporated. Chairman Al Whittaker, a member of VOC's Board of Servants, was an executive with Bristol-Myers and the Mennen Company when at age 54 he left behind his financially rewarding career to help start IIDI.

His career took him to Europe, Africa, the Far East and other developing areas. Over a period of years he became increasingly uneasy about his career and increasingly concerned about the poor. In the fall of 1971 he heard a former missionary share, in passing, his desire to see the resources of the business community applied within the church to meet the needs of the poor. He talked with the man that very day and in a few months he resigned his job and was on his way to Washington, D.C. with no money and no staff for the ministry—only a group of Christians with a united vision.

Al describes the work of IIDI:

The thing we are really all about is setting up small businesses in developing countries as a way of providing jobs for the poor. We hear a lot about hunger and its related problems, but the root of the problem is an economic condition. People don't go hungry because there isn't enough food produced. People go hungry because they are unemployed or so underemployed that they don't have enough income to buy their food. That is the problem. In order to do something to prevent hunger, we must do something to create jobs which, in turn, provide income to buy the necessities of life.

The way we create employment is by starting small businesses. By providing certain resources for the people in these countries such as technical assistance and financing, you can help them become business entrepreneurs. In the past seven years we have been able to create over 150 businesses of all types.

We presently work in four countries—Honduras, Columbia, Indonesia, and Kenya. A field director and a small staff in each country work directly with the aspiring entrepreneur in training him, providing technical assistance, and making loans available to start the business. As these businesses develop they provide jobs and a new economic base within the community. All we ask of the people we work with is that as they become successful they help someone else in the same way we have helped them.

For example, Tito is a man in Columbia who wanted to learn beekeeping. A Christian businessman from Canada went to Columbia, showed Tito how to make the hives and how to take the honey and market it. He loaned Tito $5,000 to start the business and told him he could repay in honey or in cash. For about three years Tito sent sufficient honey back to the man in Canada to pay back the entire loan. During this time Tito was teaching others the various aspects of beekeeping. According to the last report, there were five businesses that this man had generated out of his original business.

These new businesses are created within a Christian context. The love of Christ is shown in a very meaningful way through meeting a physical need.

Throughout this land, in every ghetto, in every community where the poor live, we need Christian men and women with the vision of a Robert Lavelle or an Al Whittaker to rise up. We need people to lead the way in promoting the creation of co-ops and privately owned small businesses in those very communities—dry cleaners laundromats, home cleaning services, light carpentry businesses, roofing companies, and more. This is how we can do the work of redistribution. This is how we can work for economic justice in our land.

No, free enterprise doesn't have to work just for the rich; it can be made to work for the poor too.

This is jubilee: redistribution that brings economic justice to the poor and liberty to the oppressed while proclaiming the goods news of Jesus Christ.

REFLECTION

1. On what basic principle would a truly Christian economic system be founded?
2. When measured against the biblical standard of economic justice, how well does today's American economy stack up?
3. What features of the cooperative make it a valuable tool for Christian economic development?
4. Thriftco, Dwelling House Savings and Loan, and the Institute for International Development, Inc., are all examples of Christian economic development. How are these institutions different from the secular counterparts? If a retail store, a bank, and a development corporation can all be designed and managed in a way that sharply contrasts with the world's way—in a way consistent with God's financial principles which bring justice to the oppressed—what other kinds of businesses could be operated in a similar way? Give examples of what some distinctively Christian features of such businesses might be.
5. What do you think it will take to stimulate business development in our poor communities?

18

REDISTRIBUTION: A STRATEGY FOR HERE AND NOW

As I speak in colleges and universities around the country, I often   call for redistribution. Professors and students respond, "How do I go about redistributing the wealth and goods in our society?" And the question is often asked with the implication, "If you can't tell me exactly how to do it, then your point is not valid."

I won't let people get away with that. The responsibility to develop strategies for redistribution does not rest on my shoulders alone. I cannot wait to sound the call for biblical economic justice until I have a detailed blueprint for how to achieve it.

Developing strategies for achieving justice is the responsibility of the entire Body of Christ. The task calls for a great variety of gifts, a broad spectrum of experience and training. I believe that Christian colleges, with their Christian mission and their academic resources, bear a special responsibility to develop strategies for redistribution.

I challenge you, therefore, to join with me in developing creative new strategies of achieving justice for the poor among us. I challenge our church leaders to find innovative ways the local congregation can work for redistribution. I challenge our Christian college faculties to devote their finest scholarship to developing creative models of economic development especially designed for the American poor.

I have committed myself to the task. A few others have too. But if the goal of justice for all is to be achieved in America, the evangelical church must throw itself into the battle far more wholeheartedly than ever before. In light of the demands of the gospel and the needs of our nation, nothing less will do.

This whole book is my partial answer to the question of how to promote justice in our nation. The answer to the question of redistribution actually doesn't begin with chapter 15; it begins with chapter 6—relocation. For you see, in the final analysis *there is no redistribution without relocation.* The most important thing we have to redistribute is ourselves. Justice cannot be achieved by long distance. Of course, not all are called to go; some are called to send. But our basic strategy must begin with the redistribution of skilled people. Only after people are redistributed can we employ money in ways that produce development rather than dependency. There is no real redistribution without relocation.

If we have that principle firmly in mind, we can begin to look for practical ways to redistribute our resources. On the personal level, redistribution involves two basic steps: (1) reducing what we spend on ourselves, and (2) investing what we save in projects which help to bring economic justice.

First, here are some rather ordinary ideas for simplifying your standard of living in three contexts: (1) what you can do as a family; (2) what your church can do; and (3) what an intentional Christian community can do.

Simplifying your family's economic life-style
 • Use yard space or rooftop space for a garden. Plant fruit trees when landscaping.
 • Buy food cooperatively from food outlets, farmer's markets, or discount stores.
 • Take advantage of season food. Pick fruit or vegetables and then have a canning, freezing, or jelly-making party.
 • Substitute vegetable proteins for meat. Invest in cookbooks like *Recipes for a Small Planet* and *More-With-Less*

Cookbook which feature many protein-rich, meatless recipes.
- Fast regularly.
- Set a weekly food budget. Plan menus in detail before shopping.
- Make your own baby food.
- Oppose the misuse of grain for making beer and other alcoholic beverages.
- Use fans instead of air conditioners.
- Carpool when you can. Or walk or ride a bicycle. Use public transportation and support it with your vote.
- Lower your thermostat to 68 degrees or lower in the winter and bundle up with sweaters and long underwear.
- Make dishwashing a family affair instead of using an automatic dishwasher.
- Dry your clothes on a clothesline instead of in a clothes dryer.
- Share appliances, tools, lawnmowers, sports equipment, books, etc.
- Reduce or eliminate use of paper products such as napkins (use cloth ones), paper towels, paper cups and plates. Use cloth rather than disposable diapers.
- Buy and renovate an old house in the inner city.
- Give your children more of your love and time rather than more things.
- Ask yourself how much of what you spend is for status. Eliminate those purchases. Buy things for their usefulness.
- Don't let fashions dictate your clothing purchases. Learn to make your own. Shop at Salvation Army and other thrift stores. Wear your clothes until they wear out.
- Develop less expensive, more joyful celebrations. Turn simple everyday happenings into celebrations. See the *Alternative Celebrations Catalog* (published by Alternatives, Box 20626, Greensboro, N.C. 27420) for ideas.
- Make gifts rather than buying them. Not only are handmade gifts less expensive, they are more treasured. Make your Christmas gift list in January. Budget a few dollars a month to buy gift-making materials. Make them in your spare time all year long, rather than during the Christmas rush.
- Refuse to be duped by modern gadgetry. Many modern appliances are unnecessary and energy-wasters besides.

● Avoid "buy now, pay later" schemes. They are a trap. They tempt you to live beyond your means and often lead to financial bondage. Credit, even used conservatively, is usually expensive. Pay cash and avoid paying interest.

● Reject anything which produces an addiction in you. Eliminate or reduce the use of addictive, non-nutritional drinks: alcohol, coffee, tea, colas, etc. If you are addicted to TV, sell your set or give it away. Refuse to be a slave to anything but God.

Simplifying your church's economic life-style

● Use your church building fully. Overspending on buildings wastes more American church dollars than anything else. If our churches are going to have the needed money to invest in people we are going to have to quit pouring our money into buildings. I call for churches which already own a building to postpone expansion until they are conducting four worship services. For example, a church whose auditorium seats 300 should not build until its attendance is approaching 900.

● If your church is newly organized, rent rather than build or buy, unless you will be using the building all week long for something such as a day-care center or school.

● Design all space to be multipurpose. That means, don't bolt pews to the floor. Use movable chairs. An excellent first building for a church is a gymnasium. It can be used for worship, for plays and programs, for recreation, for fellowship and dinners, and for small groups and classes. A church building is not to be a monument to anybody, not even God. It is to be a practical ministry tool.

● Organize a "things closet" in your church for things used only occasionally—tools, cots, lawnmowers, camping equipment, baby clothes, toys, etc. Church members donate or lend items to the "things closet" for others to check out as needed.

● Have regular workdays, not just at the church, but at homes. Repaint a house, weed a garden, landscape a yard, wallpaper a room, or fix up a community playground. Have a common meal at lunch time.

● Develop a Christian financial counseling ministry

within your church. Host a seminar on biblical financial principles. Send a person or couple from your church to receive training as financial counselors. These counselors can then help other church families develop specific plans for simplifying their life-styles.

● Form a baby-sitting co-op within your church. When you need a baby-sitter, you call up any other co-op family to watch your children either at your house or theirs. You "pay" for services not with money, but with co-op tokens each worth 30 minutes of child care. Co-op members meet regularly to discuss problems and update policies.

● Have a church garden plot for families who do not have home garden space.

● Families in the church can share ownership of recreational equipment and facilities. For example, three to six families could share a single vacation home, a boat, or a camper.

● Your church can collect good usable furniture and appliances for the VOC Thrift Stores or for a thrift store in your community. You can contact businesses in your community to give seconds, overruns, or damaged items from their stores to thrift stores. You can send a cash contribution to help transport these goods to the thrift store.

● Your church can take the money saved from simplifying its economic life-style and funnel it into existing Christian community development projects. But sharing your money is only the beginning; you need to also become involved in *doing* Christian community development in the very community where your church is located.

Simplifying your economic life-style through Christian community

The most important reason for Christians living together in the same neighborhood is not to save money, but for fellowship. Living together helps us to learn to know and love each other deeply. It makes it easier to truly function as a Body, ministering to each other's needs. It gives us more control over the community in which our children grow up. And Christian community brings the physical presence of Christ to a neighborhood and provides the strongest possible base for reaching out to others with the gospel.

Though secondary, financial sharing is still an important dimension of community life. Families living in community can live on far less than families living alone, and the money saved can be freed up for reaching out to the needs of the neighborhood and for supporting other worthy ministries. The very process of sharing can strengthen our spiritual unity. A community can use most of the suggestions given for families and churches, plus these ideas made more practical by the very fact of being a community.

● Share transportation. With all the families living in the same neighborhood, no family should need two cars. Some families may not need a car at all. The community can own a van for group transportation. One or two cars might be owned by the whole community to be used by anyone who needs them. Shop together to save gas.

● Share laundry facilities. Install three or four washers and a couple of dryers in a garage for the community to share. Or two or three families who live next door to each other can share a washer and dryer.

● Arrange for day care within your own community. Employ responsible young people from your community to watch your children.

● Start a tool co-op. VOC has just started one where each member pays 12 dollars a year and may check out any of the tools we have—power saws, lawn mowers, wheelbarrows, shovels, etc. The fee is used to replace tools and buy additional ones.

● Cultivate a community garden and fruit trees. Make gardening, canning, and freezing community work projects and social events.

● Cut firewood together.

● If there are older people in your neighborhood not in your fellowship who don't have access to these kinds of services, share with them. Share out of your garden, share tools, share laundry facilities, and so on. In this way your life together provides you with the resources to begin reaching out to others.

● Enjoy social activities together. Our community skates together, swims together, plays sports together, and so on. Not only does this provide inexpensive recreation and strengthen our relationships, but it is a witness for Christ in the neighborhood. Neighborhood young people see the quality of our life together—how we love one another—and they see our community and Christianity in a whole new light.

Anyone serious about simplifying his life-style at the personal, family, church, or community level will want to go far beyond these beginning suggestions. Such books as *Living More With Less* by Doris Janzen Longacre and *Living More Simply* edited by Ronald J. Sider offer a wealth of practical ideas.

Simplifying our life-styles translates into justice for the poor only as we redistribute the money saved in ways that make a difference. I believe the kind of community development which leads to meaningful redistribution includes four essential steps: (1) basic education, (2) motivation (3) vocational training, and (4) business development.

1. *Basic education.* A ministry team which relocates into a poor neighborhood will probably find inadequate public schools. I believe that the best response to this need is to create a Christian school in that neighborhood which provides an excellent education both for the children in the Christian community and for the neighborhood children.

I know that some people object, "We shouldn't waste our energy and resources developing schools; that's the government's job." Others complain, "Christian schools weaken the public school system."

But I ask, isn't it possible that the presence of quality Christian schools will strengthen the public schools by challenging them to upgrade the quality of their education?

Besides, why do we assume that schools are supposed to be run as secular rather than as Christian institutions? Is there something wrong with wanting the schools to reinforce moral values rather than to destroy them?

We need schools which teach human and spiritual values. We need schools where students can discover how their own development can result in the development of their race and of other people. We need schools that will encourage students to use their education and skills for the kingdom of God—not just for personal gain. We need schools which will produce strong Christian community leaders, leaders who can exercise responsibility wisely to bring God's hope and healing to communities crushed under the burden of sin.

The crisis our poor communities face today demands that we who live in these communities take responsibility for the education of our own children.

Can the poor community afford Christian education? The answer to that depends on how crucial we consider Christian education to be. I believe that the future of our poor communities depends on the development of strong indigenous leadership, a task at which our present school system has largely failed. If developing strong Christian leaders from among the poor is essential to breaking the cycle of poverty, then we cannot afford to *not* invest in Christian education.

Of course, operating a Christian school is a big job. Families who have just relocated will temporarily have to either send their children to the public school and supplement their education, or send them to an existing Christian school. But as soon as the Christian community has grown to the point that it can operate a school, I would encourage them to do that.

The easiest place to begin responding to the community's need for education is with a tutoring program. The next step might be a preschool or kindergarten.

To raise up strong leaders in the poor community we must provide a strong Christian education.

2. *Motivation.* Motivation grows out of education, but it goes beyond the classroom. A community can develop a monthly neighborhood newspaper that reports on community news as well as shares information and ideas useful to the people.

A low-wattage radio station that covers just your target can transmit biblical values and play Christian music. The newspaper, radio, and various community activities can become vehicles for communicating a vision of what the neighborhood can become. They can inspire hope and confidence. They can motivate people to do what they would not otherwise do.

Our leadership development program with its built-in savings plan for college or vocational school is an example of an effective motivational program. Overcoming a community's mentality by promoting personal savings is essential to motivating the poor. So a savings club or credit union will likely be one of the first economic structures you will need to create.

3. *Job training.* Obviously, in addition to basic education the poor need job skills. Once some businesses are started, these provide opportunities for on-the-job training. At Mendenhall, VOC has an Adult Education Center and classes for young people that teach employable skills. Employable skills and responsible work attitudes are clearly necessary ingredients in empowering people to fulfill their economic potential.

4. *Business Development.* Finally, the Christian community can be the catalyst for starting broadly owned co-ops or for stimulating small privately owned businesses. These businesses become in themselves vehicles for motivation and job training.

Eventually all four aspects of this task should be going on constantly in the target neighborhood. Some projects or programs will be able to achieve two or more of these goals at once. A community development program which effectively stimulates basic education, motivation, job training, and business development within the context of the gospel is achieving real economic justice.

While the church must spearhead the work of community development, other organizations can and should become partners with us in our mission. Christian colleges, Christian radio and TV stations, parachurch organizations, and even big corporations can all help.

Christian colleges
● Christian colleges can establish branch schools within the poor community, using existing facilities such as a high school, to upgrade the education of the people.

● They can establish internships to encourage students to work in existing Christian community development projects. They can create an intern class whose members spend two or three weeks volunteering in an inner city ministry.

Christian radio and TV stations
● Christian radio and TV stations can help establish small

radio and TV stations within the poor communities. These stations would not only service those communities but could become centers to train minority people for careers in the media.

● Radio and TV stations can run public service announcements for community groups involved in economic development.

Christian organizations

● Christian organizations can support various development projects. One special need is to establish more Christian schools in poor communities and to provide scholarships for students to attend those schools.

● Christian organizations can provide scholarships to train students from poor neighborhoods who are preparing to return to their homes to be Christian community developers.

● Christian organizations can invite Christian students from these poor areas to work in their ministries as interns for three to six months. During these months the student can pick up a variety of useful skills to take back to his community.

Big corporations

● Big corporations can encourage ownership among their employees through profit-sharing plans and through encouraging employees to buy company stock.

● Manufacturers and wholesalers can help retail cooperatives in poor communities get started by donating or selling at reduced rates beginning inventory and supplies.

● Big companies can provide technical assistance to cooperative groups in poor communities. They can even sell franchises to community-based cooperatives.

● Medical supply companies can provide medicine and supplies at discount prices to non-profit clinics serving poor communities.

● Clothing companies can sell seconds and overruns to retail cooperatives like Thriftco until the business becomes self-sufficient.

And these suggestions barely scratch the surface of the possibilities. Anyone who really wants to help empower the poor can find a multitude of ways to make a difference.

We must never forget that our mission is not limited to Jerusalem. It extends to Judea, Samaria, and the uttermost parts of the earth (see Acts 1:8). We must look for ways to redistribute our wealth not only at home but with the needy throughout the world. Organizations like World Vision, World Relief, Food for the Hungry, Jubilee Fund, and the Institute for International Development are vehicles for redistributing resources to the needy all over the world in Jesus' name. To share with the needy through Christian organizations, we should identify organizations which work through indigenous or relocated leaders and which are committed to a strategy of economic development rather than one of simple handouts. Of course, relief work to meet the immediate needs of the starving and homeless is necessary, but our strategy must go beyond relief to development.

Above all we must remember that our mission is not economic development alone; our mission is to take the gospel to every creature. If we moved into a neighborhood and completely wiped out poverty there but did not take the gospel of Christ, we would have failed. Economic justice demands Christian involvement precisely because it is part of the gospel. Justice is achieved when the lost hear the good news and have the opportunity to share freely in the blessing of God's creation.

Our challenge is to take the whole gospel to the whole person. Our mission is Christ's mission: "To preach the gospel to the poor . . . to proclaim release to the captives, And recovery of sight to the blind, To set free those who are downtrodden, To proclaim the favorable year of the Lord" (Luke 4:18,19).

REFLECTION

1. Whose responsibility is it to develop strategies to fulfill the biblical call for economic justice (redistribution)?
2. What single resource do we most need to redistribute?
3. What two steps does economic redistribution at the personal level involve?

THE CHALLENGE

19. Come Let Us Rebuild the Walls of America

COME LET US REBUILD THE WALLS OF AMERICA

We have looked at the needs of America, and of black Americans in particular. The needs are enormous and urgent.

We have glimpsed a vision of what can be done, of the power of the gospel to empower men for living and to restore our church and our nation to wholeness.

And we have charted a strategy for achieving that vision—a strategy of relocation, reconciliation, and redistribution.

One question remains: What kind of leader can implement this strategy? What kind of person can God use to carry it out?

Nehemiah was just such a man. Nehemiah was not a prophet. He was not a priest. He was a businessman—an administrator. With his leadership, his people rebuilt the wall of Jerusalem.

I believe Nehemiah is a model of the kind of leaders America needs today to rebuild our broken society, to bring healing to a nation sick with sin and immorality.

Nehemiah was a cupbearer for King Artaxerxes. When a group of Jews visited the capital of Persia, Nehemiah asked them how his people back home were doing. Nehemiah tells his own story:

"Now it happened . . . while I was in Susa the capital, that Hanani, one of my brothers, and some men from Judah came; and I asked them concerning the Jews who had escaped and had survived the captivity, and about Jerusalem. And they said to me, 'The remnant there in the province who survived the captivity are in great distress and reproach, and the wall of Jerusalem is broken down and its gates are burned with fire.'

"Now it came about when I heard these words, I sat down and wept and mourned for days; and I was fasting and praying before the God of heaven. And I said, 'I beseech Thee, O Lord God of heaven, the great and awesome God, who preserves the covenant and lovingkindness for those who love Him and keep His commandments, let Thine ear now be attentive and Thine eyes open to hear the prayer of Thy servant which I am praying before Thee now, day and night, on behalf of the sons of Israel Thy servants, confessing the sins of the sons of Israel which we have sinned against Thee; I and my father's house have sinned. We have acted very corruptly against Thee and have not kept the commandments, nor the statutes, nor the ordinances which Thou didst command Thy servant Moses, saying, "If you are unfaithful I will scatter you among the peoples; but if you return to Me and keep My commandments and do them, though those of you who have been scattered were in the remote part of the heavens, I will gather them from there and will bring them to the place where I have chosen to cause My name to dwell." And they are Thy servants and Thy people whom Thou didst redeem by Thy great power and by Thy strong hand.

" 'O Lord, I beseech Thee, may Thine ear be attentive to the prayer of Thy servant and the prayer of Thy servants who delight to revere Thy name, and make Thy servant successful today, and grant him compassion before this man' " (Neh. 1:1-11).

When Nehemiah heard of the plight of his people he wept and mourned for days. But his response didn't end with mourning. He let God dream in him. Then he acted on that vision. With the full cooperation of his people, the vision was made reality. The wall was rebuilt.

From this passage we can discern ten principles that

guided Nehemiah's response to the need of his people.

1. *Nehemiah prayed before he acted.* It was not until four months after he heard about the condition of Jerusalem that Nehemiah presented his plan of action to the king. It was during those four months that Nehemiah prayed and fasted on behalf of his people. And it was during those four months that God dreamed a dream in him. A God-inspired plan began to take shape. A vision grew.

During those days of prayer was laid the foundation of all that was to follow. Prayer equips us for action. Many of us tend to eagerly run out to take on the world's needs without first consulting with the One who can meet those needs. We march off to war before we get our orders. We cannot be effective in God's work unless we first get our directions from God.

Though prayer equips us for action, it is never a substitute for action. Some people respond to needs by praying and praying and praying, then walk off without ever once asking God how He can use them as part of the answer. Prayer, to be effective, must include a readiness to act. Nehemiah's prayer did. Nehemiah struck a healthy balance between prayer and action.

2. *Nehemiah sensed God's timing.* "And it came about in the month Nisan, in the twentieth year of King Artaxerxes, that wine was before him, and I took up the wine and gave it to the king. Now I had not been sad in his presence. So the king said to me, 'Why is your face sad though you are not sick? This is nothing but sadness of heart' " (Neh. 2:1-2).

Remember, now, Nehemiah heard about the need four months earlier. During those four months he had many opportunities to talk to the king, but he waited—waited for God to clearly indicate that "now is the time." Then when the time came Nehemiah didn't delay; he acted.

3. *Nehemiah counted the cost.* "Then I was very much afraid," Nehemiah said. Yet he still presented his plan to the king. Why was Nehemiah afraid? Because a servant did not have the right to be sad in the king's presence. The king's attendants were always to be happy and jovial.

About 50 years earlier, Esther needed to make a request of the king on behalf of her people. She determined, "I will go in to the king, which is not according to the law; and if I perish, I perish" (Esth. 4:16). Just as Esther faced a life or death situation, so did Nehemiah. He knew that.

But Nehemiah was afraid for yet another reason. Years before, some people had returned from Persia to Jerusalem to rebuild the Temple and the wall. They had faced opposition. Their opponents had charged that if Jerusalem was rebuilt, the King of Persia would lose control over that territory. So the king had issued a decree: "Make these men stop work, that the city may not be rebuilt until a decree is issued by me" (Ezra 4:21).

Nehemiah counted the cost. He knew he was not to look sad in the king's presence. He knew that to make his request to the king was to risk his life. And he knew that the king had issued a decree forbidding the very thing he was going to request. But having counted the cost, in spite of his fear, Nehemiah did what he had to do.

4. *Nehemiah did his homework.* "Let the king live forever," Nehemiah began. "Why should my face not be sad when the city, the place of my fathers' tombs, lies desolate and its gates have been consumed by fire?" (Neh. 2:3).

It was part of the religious tradition of Persian kings to worship their ancestors. Nehemiah knew that. So he made his appeal in the form which was most likely to win the king's sympathy: "The place of my fathers' tombs lies desolate." Nehemiah never mentioned the name Jerusalem. He never brought up the political situation.

Before Nehemiah ever made his request he planned carefully. He charted his route. He knew what letters of permission he would need for safe passage through other provinces. And he knew what materials he would need to build the wall (see vv. 7,8). Nehemiah prepared. He did his homework.

5. *Nehemiah recognized God's control.* "Then the king said to me, 'What would you request?' So I prayed to the God of heaven" (v. 4). After four months of prayer the moment of truth came and Nehemiah shot off a prayer to God. He was depending totally on God.

After Nehemiah made his requests to the king, he reported, "The king granted them to me because the good hand of my God was on me" (v. 8).

Nehemiah saw the cause and effect relationship. He

depended on the God who was in control.

6. *Nehemiah identified with his people.* Nehemiah had worked his way up into the system as high as a Jew could go. He saw the king every day. But he never lost concern for his people.

When his brothers came from Judah he asked, "How are things in Jerusalem?"

They answered, "Things are tough in Jerusalem. The people are in distress. The wall is broken down and its gates are burned."

Nehemiah didn't ask, "What kind of poverty program can I set up?" He didn't ask the king to send a construction crew. He said, "Send me."

In verse 17, Nehemiah said to the people, "You see the bad situation *we* are in." He didn't say *you;* he said *we.* 'Come, let *us* rebuild the wall of Jerusalem that *we* may no longer be a reproach" (v. 17, italics added). Nehemiah identified with his people. He relocated among them to serve them. He was one of them.

"I also applied myself to the work on this wall," Nehemiah reported later (5:16). He didn't just supervise. He worked along with all the rest.

Nehemiah didn't go to do the work *for* the people. Nor did he go just to give advice or supervision. He went to do it *with* the people.

7. *Nehemiah tested his plan.* Nehemiah went to Jerusalem. After three days he went out at night with a few men to inspect the wall. He circled the city from east to west, picking through the rubble. The rubble got so bad that Nehemiah's donkey couldn't go any further, so he got off and walked (see 2:11-15).

What was Nehemiah doing? He was rechecking his plans to see if they matched the real situation. He couldn't do this until he relocated. Testing plans against the real situation can only occur in the community of need.

8. *Nehemiah sought God's continued direction.* "I arose in the night, I and a few men with me. I did not tell anyone what my God was putting into my mind to do for Jerusalem" (v. 12).

Though God had been dreaming in Nehemiah for four

months, the plan was not yet complete. Nehemiah went ahead and took the first step—he relocated. Now in Jerusalem he was seeking God's further direction. God was putting a plan into his mind. It was only as he checked his general plan against reality that the details of the plan became clear.

We are sometimes tempted to wait until we have a complete road map before we take the first step. However, that is not how God works. We cannot know what the second step should be until we have taken the first step. Nehemiah took the first step, then continued to listen for God's direction even as he began to work. It was only after Nehemiah fully committed himself to the project, only after he was on the scene, that God's plan was fully revealed to him.

9. *Nehemiah inspired a spirit of cooperation.* "You see the bad situation we are in," Nehemiah said. "Come, let us rebuild the wall of Jerusalem that we may no longer be a reproach" (v. 17). Then Nehemiah told them how God had enabled him to return, and what the king had said. "Then they said, 'Let us arise and build.' So they put their hands to the good work" (v. 18). Nehemiah focused the attention of the people not on himself, not on the king, but on God and on the task at hand. On that basis Nehemiah recruited the cooperation of the people.

Nehemiah 3 lists 42 groups of people who are building the wall. Priests and Levites, governors and nobles, men and women, young and old, working shoulder to shoulder, side by side, to complete the task. Men came from Jericho 40 miles away to help. Nehemiah's ability to recruit the support of all these people to do the work is a powerful example of reconciliation.

10. *Nehemiah refused to let his enemies distract him.* The Jews faced constant and strong opposition throughout the entire project. Yet Nehemiah pressed on with the work single-mindedly. "The God of heaven will give us success; therefore we His servants will arise and build," Nehemiah answered his opponents (v. 20).

Though the threats were strong, God had given them a task to do. Nehemiah kept the eyes of the people on the task rather than on the threats of their enemies, and so the wall was completed.

I believe that the wall of America—particularly in our ghettos, in Appalachia, and in other poor rural areas—lies in ruins today. Our prisons are full. We don't need to build new ones; we need to empty the ones we have. Our mental institutions are full of young people who have been shot up with drugs. We don't need more institutions; we need to save our kids.

Where are our Nehemiahs who will let God dream His dreams in them? Who will sense God's timing and act neither too early nor too late?

Where are our Nehemiahs who will count the cost and still march ahead? Who will prepare themselves thoroughly for the task at hand? Then proceed in the face of danger because God is in control?

Where are our Nehemiahs who will give up the comforts of the king's court to live among their oppressed brothers and sisters, to share in their sufferings, to work together with them to bring justice to the land?

Where are our Nehemiahs who will act though the future is uncertain, who will test their plans against reality in the community of need and will let God direct their work even as they proceed?

Where are those Nehemiahs among us who will focus the attention of the people on God's power and promise and thus inspire a spirit of wholehearted cooperation? Who will not let their enemies, however ominous their threats, distract them from the task, because God has called them to do it?

I believe that throughout our nation and around the world are men and women of God whom God is calling to just such a task—young black lawyers and doctors; experienced nurses and educators; affluent white suburban managers and financiers; skilled builders and architects; middle-class plumbers and electricians; trained secretaries and journalists; students and time-tested retirees; people, whatever their gifts, whatever their skills, who are willing to be servants. "The harvest is plentiful, but the laborers are few, therefore beseech the Lord of the harvest to send out laborers into His harvest" (Luke 10:2).

I challenge you to join me in praying for workers for the harvest. And as you pray, do not let your prayer be a substitute for action; rather, pray "Lord, what would you have *me* to do?"

My fondest dream for my country is that God would raise up an army of Nehemiahs who would relocate in every community of need throughout the land, and live out the gospel that brings liberty and justice. God *can* heal our land!

REFLECTION

1. Of the 10 principles which guided Nehemiah's response, which two or three do you think are most crucial for you in carrying out the tasks God has called you to do? Why?
2. Right now, take just a few minutes to act on the author's challenge to pray for workers for the harvest, and in particular, to ask, "Lord, what would you have *me* to do?"

INTERACTION # 1—THE NEED

Activity I: Resolved . . . (10 to 15 minutes)

Two group members who have prepared beforehand conduct a debate on the topic: "Resolved, that the church is responsible to meet only spiritual needs; meeting other needs may be good and right, but it is not part of the church's mission."

Each debater may present a two- to three-minute statement of his position and a one- to one-and-a-half minute rebuttal to his opponent's statement.

Do not carry the debate over into class discussion. The purpose of this activity is not to inspire a spirit of debate, but rather to sharply define the issue to be explored during the session.

Activity II: Jesus, Our Model for Ministry (10 to 15 minutes)

Form working groups of three or four. Each group's task is to survey specified chapters of Mark's Gospel account to discover what kinds of needs Jesus was ministering to each time He met the needs of others.

Divide Mark's Gospel among the groups. For example, if there are four groups, each group will survey four chapters.

Each group should make a list of each ministry incident mentioned in each chapter, then beside each incident jot down what need(s) Jesus met. For example:

Reference	Incident	Need(s) met
Mark 1:21,22	Teaching in the synagogue	Spiritual and educational needs
Mark 1:23-27	Driving out evil spirits	Spiritual need

After six or seven minutes share with the whole group what you discovered about the kinds of needs Jesus ministered to.

Activity III: A Holistic Gospel (5 to 15 minutes)

It was through the honky-tonk episode that the author first became aware that evangelism was not enough—that the gospel called for a whole-person response to the needs of people. Can you recall a personal experience that illustrates this truth? Would you share that experience with your group?

Activity IV: Taking Christ's Mission Seriously (5 to 15 minutes)
When the author says that the gospel is holistic, he is saying that it speaks to all of a person's needs—not just spiritual needs, not just social needs. A "gospel" which addresses social needs but neglects spiritual needs is not the gospel of Jesus Christ at all. A "gospel" which addresses spiritual needs but not other needs is not the gospel of Jesus Christ. Therefore, our ministries both as individuals and churches must express the holistic nature of Christ's mission.

In groups of four, complete the following statements. Many good answers are possible.
1. If our church took seriously the holistic nature of Christ's mission, we would . . .
2. If I took seriously the holistic nature of Christ's mission, I would . . .

Close with conversational prayer in your groups of four.

INTERACTION #2—THE VISION

Activity I: What to Do? (5 to 10 minutes)
Share with your whole group or in groups of four:
Have you ever really wanted God's direction for what to do with your life, or at least a part of your life, and you just couldn't seem to hear God's voice? If so, what are some of the feelings you had then?

Activity II: Characteristics of God's Call (10 to 20 minutes)
Discuss these questions as a large group:
1. The author illustrated several characteristics of God's call from the lives of biblical people. Match each person to the characteristic or characteristics he illustrates.

A.	Abraham	a.	Felt inadequate to accept his call
B.	Ahimaaz	b.	Tried to escape God's call
C.	Isaiah	c.	Went without being sent
D.	Jonah	d.	On the verge of panic
E.	Peter	e.	Followed God's call halfway, then delayed
		f.	Called to a stubborn, insensitive people
		g.	Heard God's call a second time

2. In relation to your experience of God's call, with which of these five men do you most identify? Why?
3. The author says, "God never calls us to do something in our own strength. He always calls us to get in over our heads— to move out to where we'll have to either depend on His power, or sink." Do you agree, or do you think the author is overstating his point?

Activity III: Hearing and Obeying God's Call (10 to 15 minutes)
In groups of four, share as guided by these questions:
1. What is your best understanding of God's call on your life right now? What task is He directing you to make your priority at this time in your life?
2. Review the four steps of discerning God's call at the end of chapter 4. Where in this process are you right now?

3. What is your next step of obedience in either discerning or carrying out God's call?

Join hands, and pray around the circle, each person praying for the one on his right, particularly in relation to his next step of obedience.

INTERACTION #3—THE STRATEGY: RELOCATION

Activity I: Do We Have to Relocate? (5 to 10 minutes)

Three or four group members should prepare beforehand a short roleplay to demonstrate how the question of relocation might first arise. These dramatists will portray a church committee assigned the task of developing a strategy for a proposed new ministry to the inner city (or an appropriate needy area near your church).

One committee member may state rather matter-of-factly, "Of course, we'll have to move into the neighborhood." The response of other committee members may imply that such a suggestion is absurd. Perhaps another will honestly ask whether moving into the neighborhood is needed or even practical. Your roleplay group can take it from here with their imaginations. Here's a good place for some creative humor, poking fun at some of our own prejudices and excuses.

Activity II: Outsiders or Insiders (5 to 15 minutes)

Discuss as a group:

1. The author is convinced that ministry to the poor must be led by "insiders," by people who live among them and have been accepted as part of the community. In what ways did relocating prove to be an asset in his ministry?

2. The author also believes that programs for the poor designed and led by outsiders will usually not lead to self-sufficiency, but to dependency, actually crippling those they are designed to help. Can you give examples of how you have seen this happen? (Chapter 16 relates several such stories.)

3. How does applying the "felt need concept" relate to the issue of relocating?

Activity III: Counting the Cost (10 to 20 minutes)

Do you find yourself resisting the suggestion that relocation is necessary? If not, maybe it hasn't quite sunk in just how costly relocation is. It involves a lot more than a change of address. It means not only giving up privileges, but also voluntarily sharing the oppression of others.

1. What were some of the costs Jesus had to pay to relocate among us on earth? What privileges did He give up? What

needs and oppression did He accept as His own by becoming one of us?

2. Moses is another example of relocation (see Heb. 11:24-26). What did relocation cost him—both in terms of privileges given up and oppression accepted?

3. If some families from your church were to move into a poor neighborhood to establish a ministry, what privileges might they have to sacrifice in the process? What hardships might they have to endure or what needs might they experience as a result of identifying with the poor?

4. In chapter 9 the author writes:

> As I speak around the country, some people find my words on relocation hard to accept. They ask, "Do all have to relocate?"
>
> I answer, "Only those who are called have to relocate." Then I add, "But if you're asking the question too angrily, then you may be called. If you are uneasy about it, God may be calling you."
>
> If you resist the suggestion to relocate, you need to ask, "Why don't I want to go and live among the poor and wretched of the earth?" Ask yourself that question several times. Your answer will be the reason you ought to go."

Apply that last suggestion to yourself. What do you find most negative about the idea of relocating among the poor? Now, can you see how those negatives could be the very reasons the poor need you?

Activity IV: Ready to Go (3 to 6 minutes)

Not all are called to relocate among the poor. (Whew! What a relief!)

But—we are called to be willing to go wherever God leads us! If there is anywhere we are unwilling to go, then something else has become more important to us than obedience to God.

Silently before the Lord, examine your own heart. Are you willing to relocate among the poor if God should call you to do so? If so, express that commitment to God.

Is there something in your life so important to you that you would not give it up to obey a call to live among the poor? Ask the Holy Spirit to search your heart and to single out any such false god. Can you surrender it to God? Or at least resolve to do so soon, and ask God to give you the strength to let go of this false security?

No, God doesn't call us all to go, but He does call us all to be willing to go. As you come to God with a willing heart, your ears will be open to His call—wherever it is He is calling you.

Close your session by singing together a song of commitment such as "Ready to Go," "I'll Go Where You Want Me to Go," or "Where He Leads Me."

INTERACTION #4—THE STRATEGY: RECONCILIATION

Activity I: Naming the Walls (4 to 8 minutes)

Think of the groups of people in your own community who are divided by hostility, and name the walls that divide them. Some groups may be divided by more than one form of prejudice.

Activity II: The Gospel and Reconciliation (5 to 10 minutes)

In groups of four, read each of the following Scripture passages:

> Matthew 5:23,24
> Galatians 3:28
> Ephesians 2:14-16
> Colossians 3:11

Summarize in one sentence the main thrust of what these verses say about reconciliation with one's fellowman.

Activity III: Planning for Reconciliation (10 to 20 minutes)

Form groups of four or five.

Your church is moving toward establishing a ministry in a poor community. You will be sending a missionary team of three or four families from your church to live in that target community. Your church board has expressed the hope that from the beginning, the ministry will be a bringer of reconciliation. They want the ministering team to be a reconciled community, they want the ministry to promote reconciliation between divided groups in the neighborhood, and they want the ministry to build bridges between the people in the home church and the people in the target community.

Your small group is a committee established by the church board to draw up a list of suggested first steps to be taken to begin moving toward these goals. Feel free to borrow from chapter 14 any ideas which seem to apply to your community, but make at least half of your idea list original.

After six or eight minutes, share your list (or at least your best ideas) with the whole group.

Activity IV: Bridge-building (4 to 8 minutes)

The author has given some examples of how individuals

can take the initiative in building bridges where barriers now exist. Jot down three or four specific things you as an individual might be able to do to build bridges between divided groups in your community.

Now are you ready to go that next step and commit yourself to being an active reconciler? If so, select one of the methods of bridge-building you just listed on which you will follow through. Set a time limit within which you plan to accomplish it.

Close your session with prayer that your fellowship will be a more fully reconciled community, and that you will each be effective reconcilers in your world.

INTERACTION #5—THE STRATEGY: REDISTRIBUTION

Activity I: Exploited (10 to 15 minutes)
The author's first major lesson in economics came standing on a hay farmer's back porch when he was paid 15 cents for a full day's work. Can you think of a time when you were economically exploited? Share in groups of two or three how you felt. Why was the other person able to exploit you? What, if anything, does your experience reveal about the maldistribution of resources in our country?

Activity II: On Economic Justice and Sharing (10 to 20 minutes)
Read these five Scripture passages which deal with sharing with the poor and economic justice. Jot down the two or three concepts you find which say the most to you.
> Isaiah 58:6-10
> Ezekiel 16:48-50
> Matthew 25:31-46
> Luke 3:7-11
> 1 John 3:16-18

In groups of three or four, tell which concepts you singled out and why.

Activity III: Living More Simply That Others May Simply Live (10 to 15 minutes)
A. Quickly scan the checklist of ideas for simplifying your standard of living from chapter 18. Borrowing from this list, and adding some of your own, list six or eight ways you could reduce your cost of living in order to share more generously with the needy.

B. Name some ministries you know of which promote economic justice through relief or economic development projects. Which of these projects include at least one of the aspects of development listed in chapter 18—basic education, motivation, job training, and business development? Which of these projects are led by people who live among those they are ministering to? If you don't know, how can you find out?

Which of these ministry projects do you believe would be the best steward(s) of the money shared with the poor?

C. You can take a first step toward living more simply that others can simply live right now. From the list of cost-of-living reducing ideas in part A, select just one which you will begin to implement immediately. About how much money per week or month should this save?

Now, select one ministry project from part B with which you will share the money saved from your life-style simplification.

Decide:

1. Where will you keep the money you are saving for this project?

2. How often will you send the money from this fund to the ministry project?

Don't put off starting this project because the amount of money you will start with seems small. Even with a small amount, you can establish the habit of living with less and investing the money saved to help the needy. Once your sharing fund is established, you can find other ways to reduce your cost of living in order to put more in the fund. As your fund grows, you may want to share with several worthy ministry projects.

INTERACTION #6—THE CHALLENGE

Activity I: Group Ministry Project (30 to 50 minutes)

This is probably the single most important group learning activity in this book. If you use only one group activity, make it this one.

Before the session, the group leader—with the possible assistance of the pastor, class members, or other resource people in the church—should select two or three ministries to the poor where all interested class members could volunteer as a group. (An alternative is to design from scratch a class project through which each class member would have an opportunity to minister to the poor. This option is not as strong in helping participants catch a vision for the possibilities.) All proposed projects should involve sharing time and energy—not just money or possessions.

The group leader should outline the various proposed projects briefly, yet in sufficient detail that the group can make an informed choice of a ministry project. The group may take anywhere from 10 to 30 minutes to discuss the pros and cons of each option and to choose a group ministry project.

Once a project is agreed on, move into the planning phase. Set a date for the project. Make it as soon as practical so this study will still be fresh on your minds. Divide responsibility for preparation among group members. You may want to create working groups to plan various aspects of the project. Select a project coordinator and a steering committee who will implement the group's decisions and complete preparations for the ministry project.

Activity II: Self-offering (5 to 10 minutes)

Pray silently or conversationally for workers for the harvest among America's poor. During this prayer time group members should be encouraged to offer themselves to God to work in this ministry if God should call them to do so.

Close by singing together a song of commitment such as "Take My Life and Let It Be."

INTERACTION #7—POST-SEASON

At the close of your volunteering project before the group returns home, or shortly after the group returns home, have a group session to share what you learned through that experience. Discuss what kind of continuing response God is wanting from your group. From your church. From you. Do you need to form a group of those who are sensing a call to make a continuing commitment to the poor so that together you can shape a strategy for ministering to the poor in your community or a nearby community?

NOTES

1. Charles W. Colson, *Life Sentence* (Lincoln, VA: Chosen Books, 1979), p. 149.
2. James H. Cone, *God of the Oppressed* (New York: The Seabury Press, 1975), p. 2.
3. Paul B. Henry, *The Chicago Declaration*, Ronald J. Sider, ed. (Carol Stream, IL: Creation House, 1974), p. 138.
4. Howard A. Snyder, *The Community of the King* (Downers Grove, IL: Inter-Varsity Press, 1977), p. 107.
5. John Perkins, *A Quiet Revolution* (Waco, TX: Word Books, 1976), p. 79.
6. Martin Luther King, Jr., "I Have a Dream," 1963. Reprinted by permission of Joan Daves.
7. Cone, *God of the Oppressed*, pp. 147-48.
8. *Perkins vs. State of Mississippi*, p. 18.
9. *Perkins vs. State of Mississippi*, p. 9, 19.
10. Jean Vanier, *Community and Growth* (New York: Paulist Press, 1979), p. 26.
11. Vanier, *Community and Growth*, p. 1.
12. Claude Noel, *Serving Our Generation*, Waldron Scott, ed. (Colorado Springs: World Evangelical Fellowship, 1980), pp. 176-7.
13. Stanley Mooneyham, *What Do You Say to a Hungry World?* (Waco, TX: Word Books, 1975), pp. 207-8.
14. R. Z. Hallow, "The Blacks Cry Genocide," *The Nation*, April 28, 1969, p. 535.
15. James A. Tillman, Jr., *Why America Needs Racism and Poverty* (Four Winds, 1969), p. 254.
16. Ronald J. Sider, *Rich Christians in an Age of Hunger* (Downers Grove, IL: Inter-Varsity Press, 1977), p. 97.
17. Robert K. Hudnut, *Arousing the Sleeping Giant* (New York: Harper and Row Publishers, 1973), p. 59.